LEGENDS OF N.C. STATE BASKETBALL

TIM PEELER

www.SportsPublishingLLC.com

ISBN: 1-58261-820-8

Publishers: Peter L. Bannon and Joseph J. Bannon Sr.
Senior managing editor: Susan M. Moyer
Acquisitions editor: Dean Reinke
Developmental editor: Dave Brauer
Art director: K. Jeffrey Higgerson
Book design: Heidi Norsen
Dust jacket design: Chris Mohrbacher and Dustin Hubbart
Project managers: Jennifer Polson, Greg Hickman and Jim Henehan
Imaging: Dustin Hubbart, Chris Mohrbacher, Heidi Norsen, Kerri Baker and
        Jeff Higgerson
Photo editor: Erin Linden-Levy
Vice president of sales and marketing: Kevin King
Media and promotions managers:
        Jonathan Patterson (regional)
        Randy Fouts (national)
        Maurey Williamson (print)

Printed in the United States

Sports Publishing L.L.C.
804 North Neil Street
Champaign, IL 61820

Phone: 1-877-424-2665
Fax: 217-363-2073
Web site: www.SportsPublishingLLC.com

For Ruth Gales Peeler, and the grandsons
who never got to know her,
Michael and Benjamin.

CONTENTS

Foreword...vii

Acknowledgments...ix

Everett Case 2

C.A. Dillon 14

Dick Dickey 20

Vic Molodet 26

Ronnie Shavlik 32

Lou Pucillo 40

Eddie Biedenbach 46

Norm Sloan 52

Vann Williford 62

Tommy Burleson 70

David Thompson 80

Monte Towe 90

Kenny Carr 98

Jim Valvano..106

Dereck Whittenburg/Sidney Lowe/Thurl Bailey 118

Lorenzo Charles 128

Nate McMillan 134

Vinny Del Negro 142

Chucky Brown 150

Les Robinson 156

Fire & Ice 164

Julius Hodge..172

FOREWORD

When you work every day in a building named for Everett Case and you spend significant time walking through the hallways and on the court at Reynolds Coliseum, you can't help but soak up the tradition of N.C. State basketball.

I wasn't yet two years old when Coach Case, the man who began ACC basketball mania from his place on the Wolfpack's bench, diagrammed his last play in December 1964. But the fact that the league has endured for 50 years as the best basketball conference in the country is a tribute to his vision and success. He won 10 conference championships in his first 13 years as the coach here, and paved the way for Norman Sloan and Jim Valvano both to win NCAA championships for the school.

From the day I came to Raleigh from Miami of Ohio, I have tried to embrace that tradition, whether it be sharing ideas and coaching philosophies with the late Coach Sloan or making sure former players always feel welcome to return for games, as living—and cheering—reminders of the program's glory.

Before the men's basketball team moved its home from Reynolds to the RBC Center, Les Robinson and I wanted to make sure that some of those players were placed on their proper pedestals, which is why we pushed to honor the jerseys of All-Americans like Dick Dickey, Sammy Ranzino, Bobby Speight, Ronnie Shavlik, Vic Molodet, Lou Pucillo and John Richter. Their honored jerseys now hang in the RBC Center, along with others who have contributed all-star careers.

As I said at the time, it's good to remember the old proverb: When you drink the water, always remember who dug the well. There are many people who have invested a great deal of themselves to create N.C. State's tradition, and I think it is always a good idea to thank those people for their contributions.

When we moved to our new home at the RBC Center in 1999, we continued to remember some of the players who were the bricks in the foundation of the program's success, so in addition to David Thompson's retired No. 44 jersey, we honored some of his teammates who helped make the Wolfpack of the 1970s so dominant: Tommy Burleson, Monte Towe and Kenny Carr. We've honored others, from Dereck Whittenburg, Sidney Lowe and Thurl Bailey—the core of Valvano's 1983 championship team—to players who parlayed strong playing careers here to success in the NBA, like Vinny Del Negro and Nate McMillan to the latest honorees Chris Corchiani, Rodney Monroe and Tom Gugliotta.

Obviously, that tradition extends to more than just the players who wore the uniforms, which is why we also included Coach Case, Coach Sloan and Coach Valvano with whistles hanging from the rafters and longtime announcer C.A. Dillon with a dangling microphone.

It's always an added boost to see some of those guys sitting behind our bench when we play a tough ACC game, and it's important for old and new fans to see them as still a part of the program.

So I was excited to hear that many of them would be profiled in this collection of stories, as a reminder for those members of the Wolfpack nation who saw them play firsthand and as an introduction for those who have just begun to learn about the school's great tradition.

For some, Ronnie Shavlik's and Thompson's fantastic exploits on the court may have faded slightly over the years, but this is a great reminder of why they were such influential players in the history of ACC basketball. There are also stories about the highs and lows of N.C. State basketball, from seven-foot-four Burleson to five-foot-nine Lou Pucillo, the shortest player Case ever recruited.

There are also stories of players who survived the frustration of not playing as soon as they arrived on campus. Take a guy like Vinny Del Negro, who sat and waited two and a half years before he saw regular playing time in his career. All he did was help N.C. State win the 1987 ACC Tournament, take home the Everett Case Award as the Most Valuable Player, then spent 13 years playing professional basketball. There's Chucky Brown, who is one of the few players in ACC basketball history to win both an ACC title and an NBA title. The chapter on Julius Hodge may not be complete, since he still has a season remaining to add to his Wolfpack legacy, but the 2004 ACC Player of the Year has included his name in the long list of All-Americans and superstars who have become *Legends of N.C. State Basketball*.

Here's hoping that there will be many more to come.

—Herb Sendek
N.C. State basketball coach
2004 ACC Coach of the Year

ACKNOWLEDGMENTS

In March 1987, I was on the floor at the ACC Basketball Tournament at the Capital Centre in Landover, Maryland, covering the event for the second time as the sports editor of *Technician*, the N.C. State student newspaper. I was taking my seat on the sidelines when I saw a flashing message on the scoreboard: "Tim Peeler call home."

My grandfather, Harse Gales, had passed away, and I had to catch the next plane back to North Carolina for the funeral. While I was gone, N.C. State and Jim Valvano went on another improbable run to win the ACC Tournament title, and I wasn't there to cover it.

The funeral was in the afternoon, and as the family made the 20-mile drive from the funeral home to the church where he was buried, I was in a car with my brother-in-law listening to Wally Ausley and Garry Dornbug call the championship game between the Wolfpack and North Carolina on the radio. I felt incredibly guilty for worrying about something like this at such a difficult time for my family.

As the funeral procession pulled into the church, Vinny Del Negro hit the two free throws that sealed N.C. State's 10th ACC championship. When I rejoined my mother just before we unloaded the casket that car-ried her father, she looked at me, squeezed my hand and said, "They did it, didn't they?" She and my dad had been listening to the game in the hearse the whole time.

Like so many families across the state of North Carolina and throughout the South, we grew up watching ACC basketball games on Wednesday nights and Saturday afternoons. My mom, Ruth Gales Peeler, loved college basketball, though she never pulled for just one team. She liked whoever had the best story or whoever had in some way touched her heart.

In 2000, just before another ACC Tournament, my mom became very ill, and the doctors couldn't tell us why. She spent some time in the hospital, and in April, on my oldest sister's birthday, she was diagnosed with pancreatic cancer. She lived four months after the doctors told us the news.

One of the last things she really enjoyed before she died was one final trip to the ACC Tournament championship game. My dad, himself fighting colon cancer, dropped her off at the front door of the Charlotte Coliseum, then joined her in the stands to watch Duke whip Maryland by 23 points in a completely forgettable championship game. But for my mom, being there, awash in the electric tournament atmosphere that has captivated so many souls for more than a half century, was a chance to forget about being sick, if only for a few hours.

When I was asked to write this book, I wanted to do it for her, because she was proud of me and she was a loving fan of college basketball. Many of these are stories I have told before while working for various newspapers in North and South Carolina: *Technician*, *The Raleigh Times*, *The Salisbury Post*, *The Greenville* (S.C.) *News* and *Piedmont*, the *Durham Herald-Sun* and the *Greensboro News & Record*.

There are many people to thank for getting this volume in print. Foremost is my wife, Elizabeth Davis Peeler. She's not a basketball fan, and just about everything in this book will be news to her. But that's okay, she is still the inspiration for everything I do. Thanks to her parents, John and Nancy Davis, who are always willing to be doting grandparents when we need to work.

I want to thank my dad, Don Peeler, and the rest of my family for their continued support: Donita and Delaine Davis, and their sons John and Jeffery; Beth and Doug Finley, and their sons Matthew and Jordan. Maybe some of these stories would have made Mom smile.

There are many people to thank for the gathering of information that is included here, including current Wolfpack basketball coach Herb Sendek and his staff. In particular, Beverly Sparks, who was driven to retirement by my numerous inquiries for contact information, was as helpful during this project as she was while working for the sports information office during my student years.

N.C. State associate athletics director Annabelle Vaughan and her staff—Bruce Winkworth, Brian Reinhardt, Pat Norris, Chennelle Miller, Bill Newton, Brandon Yopp and Caffie Darden—were always willing to put up with me, and sometimes my sons, as I went through decades of files in their offices and down in the sweltering "cage" in the basement of Reynolds Coliseum. Part of the proceeds of this book will go to buy a fan for that damned place.

A special thanks goes to Frank Weedon, who was always willing to share seven or eight anecdotes about the people in this book, even if I only asked for one.

I relied on the memories of dozens of people who lived these events and many of my colleagues in the newspaper business who covered them. I dug up many of their stories from years past and talked to them to make sure I had things in proper context. In particular, Dave Droschak contributed much to this volume, including the profiles of Dick Dickey and Vic Molodet. Remembering those players from the Everett Case era and their playing days made this a richer history.

Guys like Caulton Tudor, Barry Jacobs, Al Featherston, Chip Alexander, John DeLong, Dick "Hoops" Weiss, Lennox Rawlings, Dan Collins, Bill Hensley, Bill Cole, Ron Morris, Scott Michaux, Ed Dupree, Steve Phillips, Horace Billings, Frank Dascenzo, Bob Sutton, Tom Layton, Rudy Jones, Dan Foster, Ken Berger, Ron Green, Ron Green Jr., Mike Powell, Bruce Phillips, Steve Elling, Ed Hardin, Rob Daniels, Todd Graff, Larry Keech, Bill Hass, Irwin Smallwood, Neil Amato, Jimmy Dupree,

Brian Morrison, John Dell, Tony Barnhart and Dick Vitale have helped me in many ways during the last two decades, and I appreciate everything I learned from each of them.

I wouldn't have known much at all about ACC basketball and football if it weren't for the late, great Marvin "Skeeter" Francis, who was interviewed for the Dick Dickey chapter in this book two days before he died during heart surgery on July 6, 2004, at Baptist Hospital in Winston-Salem, North Carolina. The best thing about Skeeter was that he treated me with the same dignity and respect whether I was representing a student newspaper or a national magazine. He's an irreplaceable part of ACC history, and we will all miss him.

My first newspaper job was at *Technician*, and I never had a better time than those nights of putting out the paper during one of the more dynamic times in N.C. State athletics history. I would have never made reporting a career if it had not been for Devin Steele and Scott Keepfer, the sports editors who lured me to my first reporting position with the hokiest house ad of all time. Some of the best newspaper people I ever worked with spent as much time as I did on the third floor of the old student center putting out the paper: Todd McGee, Phil Pitchford, Jeff Bender, Barry Bowden, Katrina Waugh, Madelyn Rosenberg, Suzanne Perez Tobias, Dwuan June, John Austin, Roger Winstead,

Greg Hatem, Cheryl Zerof Russell, Bruce Winkworth, David Sneed and Fritz the Monkey. Thanks to the current staff members, including editor-in-chief Matt Middleton and sports editor Austin Johnson, for upholding that strong tradition.

A special thanks to four people who encouraged me to write and pursue a career in journalism: my West Lincoln high school English teacher, Gilda Mervine; N.C. State English professors Rod Cockshutt and Dr. Robert Kochersberger; and Dwayne Walls, the writing coach who started every single critique with "Dammit, Tim. ... "

There are three written volumes about N.C. State and ACC athletics that were great foundations of knowledge in my research. I used them to double-check facts, timelines and context. The first, *The Wolfpack ... Intercollegiate Athletics at North Carolina State University*, was written in 1976 by former N.C. State professor Bill Beezley (I spelled your name right; you can't flunk me), who taught the History of American Sports class that I took years ago in Harrellson Hall. The second, *ACC Basketball: An Illustrated history*, was written in 1988 by Ron Morris and remains the bible of ACC basketball. The third, *Pack Pride: The History of N.C. State Basketball*, written in 1994 by Douglas Herachovich.

I hope this book adds a little to that history.

LEGENDS OF N.C. STATE BASKETBALL

EVERETT
CASE

For the first three-quarters of the 20th century, no one did more to promote the game of basketball than an unimposing former semi-pro basketball player from Indiana named Chuck Taylor.

Beginning in 1922 with a short little clinic he gave in Raleigh at the behest of N.C. State basketball coach Gus Tebell, Taylor zipped across the country in a big white Cadillac with a trunk full of sneakers, giving clinics and promoting his canvas Converse All-Stars, the most ubiquitous basketball shoe ever made.

So in 1946, when N.C. State decided it wanted to put its money into establishing a high-profile basketball program in an effort to revive a moribund athletics department, Raleigh *News & Observer* sports editor Dick Herbert told H.A. Fisher, the chairman of the athletics council, and J.L. Von Glahn, the athletics business manager, to go ask Taylor, the guy who knew more about the innerworkings of the basketball than anyone except maybe James Naismith.

"The best basketball coach in the country is a lieutenant commander in the U.S. Navy," Taylor told Fisher, according to a 1951 story in the *Saturday Evening Post*. "His name is Everett Case."

Taylor and Case had coached against each other while serving in the military. But their ties went further back to the fever of Indiana high school basketball, where Case had won more state championships than anyone in history. Fisher and Von Glahn went to Atlanta to interview Case, who accepted the job without ever stepping foot onto the railroad-dissected Raleigh campus. He refused to talk about salary.

EVERETT CASE

Born: June 21, 1900 (Anderson, Indiana)
High School: Anderson High School, Anderson, Indiana
Died: April 30, 1966, of myeloma (cancer of the bone marrow)
Position: Head coach
Degree: B.A., Central Normal College, 1932; Masters Degree, Southern California, 1934
Years with the Wolfpack: 1946-1964
Record: 377-134 at N.C. State; 467-124-1 in 23 years as a high school coach
NCAA Tournament Appearances: 1950, '51, '52, '54, '56
Championships: Indiana High School State Championships (1925, '29, '36, '39); Southern Conference Championships (1947, '48, '49, '50, '51, '52); Atlantic Coast Conference Championships (1954, '55, '56, '59); Dixie Classic Championships (1949, '50, '51, '52, '54, '55, '58).
Honors:
★ 1964 Inductee to the North Carolina Hall of Fame
★ 1968 Inductee into the Indiana Basketball Hall of Fame
★ 1982 Inductee to the Naismith Memorial Basketball Hall of Fame
★ Southern Conference Coach of the Year (1947, '49, '51)
★ ACC Coach of the Year (1954, '55, '58)
★ NC State whistle retired, RBC Center

"Oh, that's not important," Case told his new bosses, according to N.C. State athletics historian Bill Beezley. "I have been fortunate in my investments. Money isn't the big consideration."

Frankly, the school officials thought the school might be setting itself up for embarrassment if Case didn't take a competitive salary and a multiyear contract. Case agreed to take $5,000 per year, but refused to sign more than a year-long contract.

> # "What Everett envisioned when he came to North Carolina State was a whole basketball program that involved recruiting, coaching and promoting."
>
> [VIC BUBAS]

"If I don't like it here, I will be free to leave," Case said. "If you find you don't want me, you'll be free to replace me."

That began 18 years of service at the school that included 10 conference championships in his first 13 years.

In reality, what brought the coach to N.C. State was the hulking skeleton of steel that would later become Reynolds Coliseum. Case saw it as an opportunity to make Raleigh "The Basketball Capital of the World." Fisher and the rest of the State College administration had no problem with pouring money into basketball. Wallace Wade had built national powers on the gridiron at Duke and the University of North Carolina was about to begin its Golden Age, led by All-America football player Charlie "Choo-Choo" Justice. State College, with its decrepit Riddick Stadium, couldn't match that football success, and didn't really want to try.

A basketball program was easier and cheaper to build, since it needed only a handful of players. At most southern schools, football was king, while basketball was merely a bridge from football to baseball season and a way for the football players to stay in shape.

"You have to understand that at the time he came here, there were a lot of schools that were just made up mostly of football players, who played both sports," says Vic Bubas, who spent a decade as Case's assistant before taking the head coaching job at Duke. "There were no (basketball) scholarships then. It was really back in the days when there was no such thing as a basketball program.

"What Everett envisioned when he came to North Carolina State was a whole basketball program that involved recruiting, coaching and promoting."

Initially, Case only recruited in Indiana, where he was a high school coaching legend and demon. His first team in 1947 was made up of 10 Indiana natives who were forever known as the "Hoosier Hotshots." Among them was future Wolfpack coach Norm Sloan.

Case made the Red Terrors immediately successful. He took them on a Midwest barnstorming tour in December, beating eventual national champion Holy Cross along the way. In the three years his team—which changed its nickname to the "Wolfpack" in his second year on campus—

competed in Thompson Gym, Case literally had fans beating down the doors to watch his team play.

The fire marshal famously canceled a game against North Carolina because of fans clamoring to get into the 3,400-seat gym. A game against Duke the next season was also canceled.

When Reynolds Coliseum opened in 1949, it became a basketball promoter's dream, and Case was the biggest promoter of the sport the South has ever seen. He created the Dixie Classic—his only assistant, Carl "Butter" Anderson, came up with the name—the three-day basketball marathon that was the foundation of Case's popularity with fans, with players, with opposing teams and even with officials.

Case's success forced North Carolina to hire New Yorker Frank McGuire to build a program at Chapel Hill. McGuire won the 1957 NCAA Title, the first by an ACC team, which forced Duke to go after someone who could compete with the Tar Heels. Duke athletics director Eddie Cameron hired Case assistant Vic Bubas, who eventually gave way to Bill Foster. Both took the Blue Devils to the Final Four, but it wasn't until Tom Butters hired Mike Krzyzewski in 1980 that Duke had its own dynasty-builder to eclipse all the schools' other successes. Krzyzewski sat through two horrific losing seasons while both Carolina and State won national championships in 1982 and '83, respectively, but he's done pretty well since then.

For some, that line of ascension might be convoluted, since it bounces off every exit ramp of Tobacco Road. Case wouldn't mind. He loved the school that hired him, but he really wanted to ignite passion in the game, similar to what he grew up with in Indiana.

"You have to realize that Carolina and Duke and the others were forced to improve (because of Case)," said the late Jim Valvano in a 1982 interview. "Everett had beaten Carolina something like 15 straight times at one point. I asked Frank McGuire was it true that he was hired at UNC to beat Case. He said yes, without question."

In fact, McGuire broke UNC's longest losing streak to its chief rival in his very first game against Case.

In front of fans, Case and McGuire pretended to be mortal enemies. In reality, they were friends conjoined by their love of basketball. They frequently met for dinner at the old College Inn, joined by assistants Press Maravich, Vic Bubas and Dean Smith. They would all retire to Case's home on Daniels Street in Cameron Village, to share late-night stories and Early Times whisky.

"It was always so much fun listening to those two talking about the old days," Smith says now. "It's hard when you are rivals, you have to work at (having a friendship). And they did.

"I remember when I became the head coach, after all the gambling scandals, Everett called me and I went over to his house by myself. He had his houseboy go get dinner for us, and we were talking about how tough it was going to be, with all the restrictions that were placed on the two schools, by not being able to go out and recruit. He said, 'I bet Vic (Bubas, then the Duke coach) and Bones (McKinney, the Wake Forest coach) are laughing their heads off.'"

Many people sat with Case in his living room to talk about basketball. He shared a friendship with the media and opposing coaches that is a relic of a different era. He just loved being around people who loved basketball.

"I remember one time we were there and there was this man from Raleigh who bred show dogs," said Norm Sloan, who always honored his old coach whenever he could. "He was a big basketball fan, too. Coach Case warned him, 'I don't want to talk about those damned dogs. If you don't want to talk about basketball, I don't want you to come back to my house anymore.'"

Case loved the sport, but he neither played it in high school nor was particularly good at coaching the Xs and Os of the college game. That's why he always surrounded himself with knowledgeable assistants, like Anderson, Bubas, Lee Terrill and Maravich.

"He wasn't a great game coach, but he attracted great people," says Bucky Waters, who played for Case in the 1950s and was the head coach at West Virginia and Duke later on. "He was more of a facilitator and a promoter. He would keep up with the game, and when someone like Oscar Robertson signed at Cincinnati, he immediately locked that school into playing in the Dixie Classic his senior year.

"He was just ahead of his time in terms of putting on a show."

He introduced some Indiana high school traditions to college basketball, like cutting down the nets after winning tournaments and turning down the lights during player introductions. He was one of the first coaches in college basketball to have summer camps for players, and he devised the box score that showed game stats. He once had his players warm up for games wearing flashy capes.

Never married, Case adopted his players as his sons, and like any good patriarch, left most of his money to them in his will. Case's divided $69,525 of his quarter-million-dollar estate into 103 shares, which he spread among the 57 living Wolfpack players who had earned their degrees from N.C. State.

> "He wasn't a great game coach, but he attracted great people. He was more of a facilitator and a promoter."
>
> [BUCKY WATERS]

That money came in handy to young men who weren't too far removed from college. Lou Pucillo remembers putting his three shares into his business. Waters, whose young son had a severe allergy to milk, used it to pay bills for his family. "The soy bean milk was off the chart," Waters remembers. "I was making like $5,000 a year, and that stuff was 70 cents can, and he was using three cans a day. So it didn't go into a convertible or anything like that. It was a godsend." Case put the rest of his estate, some $198,000, into a trust for his only sister,

Blanche Etta Jones, who was living with him in Cameron Village at the time of his death.

"I don't think the general public knows just how much his boys meant to Case," his neighbor, Fred Jones, told Whitey Kelley of the *Charlotte Observer*, when Case's will was made public. "His was more of a father-son relationship than it was a coach.

"A phone call or a visit from Vic Bubas always turned him on like an electric light, even when he was sick in those last days."

The only girl who ever really stole Case's heart was Beverly Shavlik, the young wife of Wolfpack star Ronnie Shavlik. Case was best man at their wedding, and he insisted that they hold the wedding reception at his home.

"Mother was mortified," Beverly Shavlik said. "But it was the perfect place. I just adored him, and all of his players were his sons."

Case never played high school basketball himself, but it was always his intention to coach. He said so in his 1919 Anderson (Indiana) High School yearbook. He began coaching at the age of 18, after attending enough weekend and night school to get his teaching degree. He strung the rest of his undergraduate degree among six different colleges during the next 13 years, as he moved from town to town coaching high school basketball teams. He settled in Frankfort, Indiana, to become head coach of the Hot Dogs. After taking Frankfort to its second state title, in 1929, he accepted the trophy from Dr. James Naismith, the inventor of the game.

Recruiting scandals dogged Case even in high school, because he was always willing to offer a promising player's father a job around town if that player's family would pick up and move to Frankfort. He finally got his college degree from Central Normal College in Danville, Indiana, in 1933.

By the mid-1930s, opponents were onto Case, and jobs were scarce everywhere. He took off for the West Coast, ostensibly to go to graduate school at the University of Southern California, where he was an assistant coach to Sam Barry. Always consumed by basketball, Case's masters thesis was titled "An Analysis of the Effects of Various Factors on the Accuracy of Free Throws." Case found the underhand shot to be the most effective, which may explain why Sam Barry's son, Rick, used that particular shot throughout his NBA career, the last professional star to use the underhand free-throw shooting method. Barry made more than 90 percent of his free throws in seven of his last eight NBA seasons.

Case went back to Indiana in 1935, and immediately won his third state title in with the Frankfort Hot Dogs. Case also began to dabble in several businesses that allowed him to never worry about what his coaching salary was. He opened a California-style drive-in called the Campus Castle in Frankfort. He began selling calendars and All-America certificates around the state, helping him earn the nest egg he lived off of for many years. Case always dabbled in stocks, frequently tipping his players to run transactions from his office in Reynolds Coliseum to his stock broker in downtown Raleigh. Lou Pucillo says that Case also considered going into the restaurant business in Raleigh. In 1959, Case wanted to bring

"He is the one who brought basketball to the ACC. After World War II, he went there and dominated, and that's what made other teams want to build up to him."

[JOHN WOODEN]

Raleigh's first McDonald's franchise to Hillsborough Street, but negotiations broke down when Ray Kroc's people wouldn't let the coach call his restaurant "Everett Case's McDonald's."

Case's final high school coaching victory came in the 1942 state tournament, when the Hot Dogs beat South Bend Central and a coach named Johnny Wooden. Some 32 years later, after Wooden had become the "Wizard of Westwood" and won seven consecutive national championships at UCLA, one of Case's pupils, Sloan, ended Wooden's domination of college basketball.

Wooden remembers the fierceness of going against Case in those cut-throat high school tournament games. And he knows what Case meant to the game of college basketball in the south.

"He is the one who brought basketball to the ACC," Wooden says. "After World War II, he went there and dominated, and that's what made other teams want to build up to him. That's why North Carolina brought Frank McGuire down from New York."

Wooden also remembers that Case built his program by nabbing some of Indiana's finest talent, just, as some people might say, like he did when he was coaching at Frankfort.

"I understand that when his players came on the floor, the opposing band would start playing 'Back Home Again in Indiana,'" Wooden says.

Case entered the navy just before World War II and spent the war years coaching military teams at various bases. He had just about decided to retain his officer's commission when Taylor put him in touch with the N.C. State athletics officials.

After he established his Wolfpack program, Case didn't just limit himself to Indiana boys. He went to New Jersey and Philadelphia, and he widened N.C. State's and the ACC's recruiting base from coast to coast when he went to Denver, Colorado, to snare six-foot-nine center Ronnie Shavlik.

Case had his quirks. Every afternoon during his tenure at N.C. State, without exception, he took a nap. He said he wanted to be well rested for retirement. He probably drank too much. He once cracked several ribs when he fell into the newly installed pool in his backyard, and forbade any of his writer friends to tell the story because he thought people would surmise he was drunk when he did it. Which was probably the case.

He may have loved his surrogate sons, but he was a gruff old bastard. "Hey, boy..." was a term of endearment. He threatened them with a boogie man he created named "Ol' Joe Hayes," who lay in the dark corners of Hillsborough Street looking for basketball players going astray.

He encouraged his players to take advantage of a free education and wanted all of them to be successful once they were out of school, but he also made them understand what was important when March rolled around.

"I remember Smedes York, who was a civil engineering major, coming into practice a little late during the week of the ACC Tournament, because he had a lab," says Les Robinson. "He comes walking in about an hour late, with his slide rule still in his pocket, which he had done all year long."

"York, what the hell are you doing?" Case yelled.

"I was in my lab, Coach," he replied.

"This is tournament week, boy. Forget all that crap!"

But as much as he loved the game, he was so burned by feuds and NCAA investigators that he discouraged some of his brightest players from following his path into coaching. Shavlik once told Abe Goldblatt of the Norfolk, Virginia, *Virginian-Pilot* that Case discouraged him from ever going into coaching. "Case told me not to go into coaching. He said it was a tough way to go, like playing a fiddle in a band. He said it didn't offer much remuneration."

Mel Thompson, Vic Bubas, Robinson and Eddie Biedenbach couldn't be convinced: they all went into coaching and were success-

ful. Coaches who followed much later around the ACC, from Jim Valvano to Dean Smith to Mike Krzyzewski might disagree nowadays about the financial rewards of the profession.

Case had his troubles, too, which he mostly blamed on his decades-long feud with Kentucky coach Adolph Rupp. State was put on probation in 1955 for illegally trying out players. Two years later, the Wolfpack was slapped with the NCAA's harshest penalty to that time, for the recruitment of a Louisiana schoolboy named Jackie Moreland. All N.C. State sports were barred from NCAA postseason competition for four years. That prevented Earle Edwards's first ACC championship football team in 1957 from accepting a bid to the Orange Bowl, the only time in school history that the Wolfpack has been invited to one of the major bowls.

"The NCAA rules are like your income tax," said Case, who never particularly liked either one. "You need an adviser to tell you what's going on with your income tax and you need an adviser to tell you what is going on with the NCAA. The NCAA has got a million rules and they have caught me on every one."

Generally, Case would claim he had no knowledge of the rules he was breaking, a claim few people at the time believed.

"I think," said a longtime friend long after Case's death, "that Ev was such a competitor, he wanted to win so much, he was willing to overlook rules in order to win."

Those infractions never bothered him nearly as much as the gambling scandals of the early 1960s, because the latter had to do

"The scandals devastated him. For a man to whom basketball was his whole life and to whom loyalty meant everything, that scandal was just total devastation."

[NORM SLOAN]

with his own players doing something to hurt the program and the game. Case had repeatedly warned his players to stay away from shady characters. He brought in SBI agents to talk to his team about it. He made all his players sign a sheet saying they had read a scrapbook full of clippings about the point-shaving scandals of the early 1950s, which forced several Northeast colleges to disband their basketball programs completely.

But four of Case's players, including captain Stan Niewierowski and Don Gallagher, the 1960 winner of the Alumni Athletic trophy, confessed to point-shaving and cooperated with investigators during college basketball's second big brush with the seedy underworld of gamblers. Case brought the investigators in himself to look into the program.

"The scandals devastated him," Sloan said in a 2003 interview. "For a man to whom basketball was his whole life and to whom loyalty meant everything, that scandal was just total devastation."

In an address to the team after the point-shaving allegations were made public, Case told his players to "buck up and fight."

"This is not a time to run or quit, but to stand up and face the issue," he said. "Naturally, this is a disappointment, but it is not the first disappointment you have ever had, nor will it be the last. In the future, you will have many disappointments that you will have to face up to. I am an optimist and have faith in the future. Do not feel sorry for yourselves, but buck up and fight, and be ready to do the things necessary. If you cannot meet the challenge now, you will not be able to do so later in life, when you will face more vital issues and disappointments."

William Friday, the president of the Consolidated University of North Carolina system, insisted that the Dixie Classic, Case's favorite event, be canceled because of the influence of gamblers and organized crime at the time.

"That had to be done because of gambling and the threats on human life, which no administrator can fail to deal with," Dr. Friday says. "I was left no option. It had to be done. By all odds, it was the most exciting basketball competition in the United States at the time. But that had to be done. That decision had to stick."

Case's last honor came in 1965, when the Wolfpack upset Bubas's sixth-ranked Duke team in the ACC Championship game. The players lifted a frail Case up to the rim to cut the final strand of net down, the tradition he brought from his Indiana high school days.

The competitive fire of basketball never left Case, even after health problems forced him to retire two games into the 1964-65 season. A week after he turned the reins over to Press Maravich, Case took a 10-day trip to Gainesville, Florida, to visit Sloan, who was the head coach at Florida at the time.

"We happened to be getting ready to play North Carolina," said Sloan, who succeeded Maravich. "He came to practice every day. The day before the game he said, 'Hey, boy, in the ACC we can't give out scouting information on other schools. But, by God, they can't play against a zone.'

"To his everlasting credit, he was a builder of men."

[JESSE HELMS]

"He was loyal to the league, but he was loyal to me, too. It was one of the highlights of all the time I spent with him."

Case died on April 30, 1966, at his apartment. He had two final requests that show both his competitiveness and the loyalty to his players. Just before he died he asked that part of his estate, $69,525, be divided into 103 shares and distributed in portions to a total of 57 former players.

The second was to be buried on a hill, overlooking Highway 70, the main road out of Raleigh in those days, so he could wave to his team as it went off to play Duke, North Carolina and Wake Forest. To this day, every time Pucillo, who with John Richter was Case's last All-Americans, honks his horn when he passes by the cemetery, and says "Thanks, Coach."

In a televised eulogy, a pre-political Jesse Helms said this of his longtime friend during one of his weekly commentaries on Raleigh's WRAL-TV:

"To his everlasting credit, he was a builder of men," Helms said. "It is a bit ironic that those who pay him due tribute as a great coach may fall short in assigning him the proper credit as a man who knew how to make dreams come true. Everett Case's eyes were fastened on something greater than the flashing scoreboard in a frenzied coliseum.

"He was able to see things in a larger perspective than many of the men around him."

He not only saw a wider perspective, but a lasting one, too. The fever for college basketball burns as bright along Tobacco Road as it did during the heyday of the Dixie Classic.

Case's legacy is still seen in the driveways across the state and throughout the South, where he himself rode the back roads in a big Cadillac that was given to him by Wolfpack supporters. That legacy is celebrated every spring, with an event called March Madness, when conferences put on their biggest money-making shows of the year with postseason tournaments and

"You have to trace everything about ACC basketball back to him. He was indeed a great salesman."

[VIC BUBAS]

teams cut down the nets following championships.

Those are both traditions Case introduced to the South, as he tried to inject the fervor of the Indiana high school game into the moribund college game everywhere south of Kentucky.

Did he succeed? Ask every athlete of the 83 NCAA-sponsored sports other than men's basketball. Roughly 98 percent of the money used to pay for annual championships for all of those sports comes from the 11-year, $6 billion deal the NCAA struck with CBS in 1999 to televise March Madness. Certainly,

Case doesn't get all the credit for that—names like Naismith, Phog Allen, Henry Iba, Wooden, even Case-nemesis Adolph Rupp, all come into play—but the program he established in Raleigh just after World War II is the genesis of ACC basketball and the league's domination of college basketball for more than a half a century.

"You have to trace everything about ACC basketball back to him," Bubas said. "He was indeed a great salesman."

And the product he sold is attracting more consumers than ever before.

C.A. DILLON

Undoubtedly, Reynolds Coliseum has a soul, one that is not just rooted in basketball. The old building is also an armory that once had an ice-skating rink. For years, it hosted Raleigh's social elite at Friends of the College concerts and it rocked to the likes of Bob Dylan and Van Halen.

But in its half century of service for men's basketball games, the versatile old building only had one voice, one that tipped off every introduction with the understated, "Good evening, ladies and gentlemen, and welcome to William Neal Reynolds Coliseum. Tonight North Carolina State University is pleased to host the basketball team from ... "

For the entire time that Wolfpack men's basketball team played in the coliseum, Clyde Alvin Dillon Jr. worked the public address system. To make it simple, Wolfpack fans always just said, "We got C.A. on the P.A."

C.A. Dillon never scored a point, but his tinny voice on the crackly sound system is as much a part of N.C. State basketball lore as Everett Case, David Thompson or Fire and Ice, because of he spans every generation of the last half-century.

"Hearing his voice is like the ghost of Everett Case," longtime N.C. State sports information director and associate athletics director Frank Weedon says.

Dillon was still a student at N.C. State in 1946, when Case arrived to lead the basketball program. Rejected by the army, Dillon enrolled at N.C. State to pursue a mechanical engineering degree, something he hoped would be helpful when he took over the fam-

CLYDE ALVIN DILLON

Born: May 26, 1952 (Raleigh, North Carolina)
High School: Broughton High School, Raleigh, North Carolina
Position: Public address announcer for basketball, football and baseball; Radio color announcer, 1958-59.
Degree: B.S., Mechanical engineering, 1946
Years with the Wolfpack: 1946-1999
Arenas: Thompson Gymnasium, Raleigh Memorial Auditorium, Reynolds Coliseum, Entertainment and Sports Arena
Honors:
★ President, Dillon Supply Company, 1971-90
★ NC State Board of Trustees, 1973-83
★ President, NC State Alumni Association, 1970-71
★ Campaign Chairman, Wolfpack Club
★ Vice President, Kiwanis International, 1990
★ Trustee Emeritus, Greensboro College
★ Board of Trustees, Southeastern Jurisdiction, YMCA
★ Governor, Carolinas District, Kiwanis International, 1985-89
★ Sports editor, *Technician*, 1944-46
★ Search committee member for hiring Lou Holtz, Bo Rein, Monte Kiffin, Chancellor Joab Thomas, Chancellor Bruce Poulton
★ Microphone retired, RBC Center

ily business, Dillon Supply Company, which his father began in 1914.

But Dillon also had his hobbies, sports and radio broadcasting. He mixed the two while in college, and became the sports editor of *Technician*, the school's student newspaper. That's where he became friends with Case, who put Dillon behind the microphone at Reynolds and behind the wheel of Case car on the road.

"I used to drive him and (assistant coach) Butter Anderson to games all the time to see Duke, Carolina or Wake Forest play," Dillon says. "We always had our seats at their gyms, and I would go by after practice to pick them up. One time, however, we got into a snowstorm in Chapel Hill and the car slid off the road into a ditch.

"He didn't let me drive in the snow any-more after that."

But there were only a few times anyone could pry the microphone out of his hands. He didn't do every game played at Reynolds, but you wouldn't need many hands to count the ones he missed. His announcing career began with Case's debut at N.C. State, a 63-28 victory over the Cherry Point Marines in December 1946, at Thompson Gym.

He called the points when Vic Bubas scored the first basket at Reynolds Coliseum, and he made the announcement to the crowd that day in 1974, after he had heard from doc-tors at Rex Hospital that David Thompson would be fine. As 12,400 fans cheered uproar-iously, Dillon was never so happy to spread some good news.

Dillon wrangled two leaves from the army, while stationed at Camp Pickett in Virginia and Fort Meade in Maryland, so he could come back to announce the Dixie Classics in 1950 and '51. He missed a game in 1956 when he was on his honeymoon, and in 1961 when his mother died. In later years, games sometimes conflicted with his Tuesday night Bible study and he sometimes had to go out of town on business.

But for 53 years, in four different build-ings, Dillon was almost always behind the mike. He started while still a student, when the team played in 2,500-seat Frank Thompson Gymnasium and went with the team when the size of the crowds dictated games be moved to the old Raleigh Memorial Auditorium. He did almost all the games—varsity, freshman, Dixie Classic, Southern Conference Tournaments, ACC Tourn-aments and NCAA Tournaments—for five decades at Reynolds. He even spent decades as the public address announcer for football games at Carter-Finley Stadium.

Ceremoniously, he did the very first game at the Wolfpack's new home, then switched off his microphone, hung up his red blazer and stopped worrying about how to pronounce the name of every player on the court. But he's such a part of the history of Wolfpack basketball, the school hung a ban-ner honoring his service right along with David Thompson, Ronnie Shavlik and all the other legends whose names he called so many times.

His banner doesn't have a number. It has an old-style microphone stitched in red and white.

Dillon has a million memories from his days on press row, which he shared with a handful of characters who showed up, almost without fail, for every game. There was Johnny Holmes, a Raleigh policeman who was the official timekeeper for decades. And Weedon, the fiery sports information director and assistant athletics director who once fired Dillon and former Raleigh mayor Jim Reid as part-time Wolfpack radio broad-casters when Weedon developed the Wolfpack Sports Network in 1961. They were replaced by Wally Ausley and Bill Jackson on Raleigh station WPTF, which is still the flagship station for Wolfpack sports.

But Dillon has never let Weedon forget about that long-ago pink slip.

For more than 35 years, Dillon sat right beside another N.C. State legend whose name has faded except for some old-timers who remember his shiny dome gleaming at mid-court. But he scored more points than anyone in Wolfpack basketball history.

Shavlik? Thompson? Monroe? No way. You could combine their career scoring totals and multiply by 100, and that total still wouldn't come close to the points scored by Duma Bledsoe.

"He kept all the points and kept them straight."

[C.A. DILLON]

Bledsoe, a stoic Raleigh businessman, kept the scorebook at Reynolds Coliseum for more than four decades, before retiring in 1985. He started in 1942, long before Everett Case arrived as head coach, and was there for much of the Jim Valvano era. He once estimated that he was the official scorer for some 750 games at the arena.

"He kept all the points and kept them straight," Dillon says.

Bledsoe used his old No. 2 pencil to record the 57 points Thompson scored against Buffalo in 1974 and the 55 points Shavlik scored against William & Mary in 1954. He put little notches in his book for the biggest names in college basketball, like Oscar Robertson, and the littlest, like Spud Webb.

He always gave Dillon a hard time. When Minnesota came to the 1954 Dixie Classic, the Gophers had a guy named Stepanovich on the team. Dillon kept repeating the proper pronunciation in his head, "Ste-PAHN-o-vich, Ste-PAHN-o-vich," while Bledsoe kept whispering in his ear "Step-a-NO-vich, Step-a-NO-vich." Dillon even remembers the time he nearly got chased from the scorers table by referee Lennie Wirtz.

"One night, Lennie Wirtz was calling the State-Duke game and it seemed like every foul that was called was on State," Dillon once told Gerald Martin of the *Raleigh News & Observer*. "Frank Weedon was sitting near me and finally, after about 10 or 12 minutes, a foul was called on Duke. Frank said to me, 'That's just the first foul. Just the first.' For some reason, it was in my head and I said, "The foul is on so-and-so, and that's JUST the first! Lennie came over there and looked at me and I said, 'I'm sorry. I'm sorry.' He said, 'One more like that and you are out of here.'"

In his years, Dillon served his alma mater in many other ways than just being a P.A. announcer. He also worked with football, and filled in on more than a few radio broadcasts. He was the main fundraiser for the Wolfpack Club in Wake County for years, and even served on the search committee when the school hired a young football coach named Lou Holtz to take over the program in 1972.

He always sat in his red blazer or red sweater at the scorer's table, but he also managed to maintain cordial relationships

"I always told him that I was going to wait until after he left. And sure enough, he retired first. I outlasted him."

[C.A. DILLON]

with coaches throughout the league. In the final years of Reynolds, whenever North Carolina played the Wolfpack, Tar Heel coach Dean Smith would wander by at some point and say, "Are you still here? When are you going to retire?"

"I always told him that I was going to wait until after he left," Dillon said. "And sure enough, he retired first. I outlasted him."

He also outlasted Case, Press Maravich, Norm Sloan, Jim Valvano and Les Robinson before handing over his mike. But Dillon's voice, and his trademark introduction, will echo throughout Reynolds Coliseum as long as the old basketball home stands on campus.

DICK
DICKEY

Dick Dickey was easy to overlook as a high school senior in Indiana in the 1940s.

The skinny redheaded guard was five foot nine and weighed 150 pounds, and liked to play defense. Not exactly what the big-time colleges were looking for back then.

But World War II turned into sort of a blessing for his basketball career. In the first six months of navy pre-flight training, Dickey grew four inches and put on 35 pounds of muscle.

He also worked on perfecting a shot that would help revolutionize college hoops in the South after he was recruited to North Carolina State by Everett Case, the former Indiana high school coaching legend.

While Dickey's navy buddies looked forward to weekend liberty, Dickey would head to the gym to work on his one-handed jumper, a shot few used back in the day.

Dickey picked up the one-handed shot fooling around in the gym and kept perfecting it. He didn't know he was on to something special until he got to Raleigh.

"In the country of the Midwest during the war we didn't have much available as far as seeing other ball players," Dickey says. "That shot seemed to work to my advantage so I stayed with it."

"People in the South were still shooting free throws underhanded and using a two-handed set shot," adds Bill Hensley, the former sports information director at N.C. State and Wake Forest. "But Dickey could really pop that one-handed jumper."

Dickey first ran across Case during two navy all-star basketball exhibition games.

DICK DICKEY

Born: October 26, 1926 (Alexandria, Indiana)
High School: Pendleton High School, Pendleton, North Carolina
Degree: B.S., Agricultural and Life Sciences, 1950
Position: Forward
Number: 70 (honored)
Years with the Wolfpack: 1947-50
Championships: Southern Conference Championship (1947, '48, '49, '50)
Honors:
★ Three-time All-America selection
★ Four-time Southern Conference all-conference-player (1947, '48, '49, '50), only four-time all-conference selection in NC State history
★ Played for four Southern Conference champion teams
★ 1949 Dixie Classic Most Valuable Player
★ 1950 Alumni Athletic Trophy winner
★ 1950 All-Final Four team selection
★ First Wolfpack player drafted into the NBA, chosen by the Boston Celtics in 1950

Case was coaching a team from Iowa, while Dickey was on a team from California. That's when Dickey realized Case would do anything to get an edge.

After Case won a close first game in Iowa, he headed to the West Coast for a rematch with Dickey's team, which had won 29 consecutive games. However, things weren't as evenly matched as when the two met on Case's home turf.

"When they came out to California he didn't play us on the base," Dickey says. "He got us on a neutral court. He told me later he didn't want to play in front of 7,000 raving, yelling cadets."

Case beat Dickey's team by a point off the base.

"Coach Case did you well if you did the right thing and played ball and didn't buck the system. He knew I wanted to win badly and so did he."

[DICK DICKEY]

When the war ended, Dickey returned home to Indiana and was set to attend Purdue. But the Midwest school didn't offer him any scholarship money, and Case won the recruiting battle.

The two immediately hit it off when Dickey began practice in Raleigh.

"He was one of Everett's favorites," said Marvin "Skeeter" Francis, the former publicity director for the Atlantic Coast Conference. "He was a scorer and Everett liked him because he was flashy. And he was good."

"Coach Case did you well if you did the right thing and played ball and didn't buck the system," Dickey says. "He knew I wanted to win badly and so did he."

Dickey, who played forward at State at 6-1, soon became a key part of Case's fast-paced offensive machine.

And his teammates didn't take long to begin to mimic his one-handed jumper in practice.

"Case put some plays in for me because I could get that shot off," Dickey says. "It was one of the ways I could get open, and I had fairly good jumping ability, so I could get over people.

"When we were playing in New York one time, a magazine took a series of pictures of my jump shot. The reaction was the whole team wanted to work on using my jump shot."

Dickey, also a high school and college high jumper, averaged 12.1 points as a freshman in 1947 on the first of four straight Southern Conference championship teams. A season later, N.C. State got 15.5 points a game from Dickey and rolled to another Southern Conference crown before a loss to DePaul in the first round of the NIT.

Dickey watched that NIT loss from the sideline because of the mumps.

"We would have played a different type of ball game if I was in there," Dickey says. "We used to press all over the court, that whole year for the whole game. Coach Case elected not to do that when I got the mumps, and we lost."

N.C. State also lost out on a chance to play in the NCAA Tournament that season, failing to get a bid despite one of the best records in the nation.

Dickey thinks he knows why.

"To get into the Final Four back then was pretty tough," he says. "We were 29-2 at the time they selected and didn't even get a bid. Mr. (Adolph) Rupp was on the selection committee, and we were in the same district as Kentucky so that may have had something to do with it."

> **"You always like when fans follow you. When I first got to Raleigh there wasn't that much activity. It was just after the war and people didn't care about basketball that much."**
>
> [DICK DICKEY]

Dickey's junior year was filled with problems. He suffered a calf injury early in the season at Nevada and broke his nose later in the year against Virginia. Still, he played in 30 of the team's 33 games and averaged 11.8 points.

"I got put up into the stands in Reno and I didn't even practice that year," he said. "It would take about three days for my calf to go back down to its normal size. I was kind of glad to see that season get over with."

Dickey's final season proved to be a magical one.

N.C. State opened Reynolds Coliseum, beat defending NIT champion San Francisco and advanced to the Final Four for the first time in school history. Fans flocked to one of the best arenas in the nation to see Dickey and Sammy Ranzino race up and down the court, firing jump shots.

"For three years we watched that skeleton out there," Dickey says of Reynolds Coliseum. "I was really beginning to think we weren't going to get into it.

"You always like when fans follow you. When I first got to Raleigh there wasn't that much activity. It was just after the war and people didn't care about basketball that

much. Plus we were all new. Nobody recognized anyone. But it sure came around during that 1950 season."

The Final Four back then was hardly the Super Bowl-style spectacle it has become. In fact, N.C. State walked from its hotel in Manhattan to Madison Square Garden for games and the only television coverage was local in New York. But it was still a big stage, and Dickey said the Wolfpack was more than prepared under Case.

"We had played in New York ever since my freshman year, so we were used to that," he says. "And we had played against good ball players from all over."

N.C. State beat Baylor and Holy Cross before losing to eventual national champion City College of New York in a close game. The highlight of that Final Four trip for Dickey was beating Holy Cross and its first-team All-American Bob Cousy.

"With the way the referees let people get by with palming the ball and everything else, there is no telling what he could have done today," Dickey says of the star guard who later became his teammate with the

Boston Celtics. "He sure had a lot of moves and didn't palm the ball or carry it."

Dickey played in N.C. State's first Final Four and was indirectly responsible for the team's second trip in 1974, convincing then coach Norm Sloan to take a chance on another Indiana player: five-foot-seven Monte Towe.

Sloan wasn't too pleased to find out that Dickey was recommending a player who was so tiny.

"I said, 'Look at the pub you're going to get. You have Tom Burleson at 7-5 and Monte at 5-7,'" Dickey says.

N.C. State ended up winning the national title with Towe as its diminutive point guard.

Dickey was the first N.C. State player drafted in the NBA, going to Baltimore. However, he was sold to the Celtics during a preseason training series in New England in 1951.

"I went up there with one team and came back with another," he says.

But like with so many of Case's stars from Indiana, Dickey didn't pan out in the pros. He soon left the team for real life.

"I really wasn't playing much and the money wasn't like it is now," Dickey says. "I was making a little over the minimum of $4,500. I would have stayed there and gotten splinters for the minimum salaries they have now, but I just walked in and quit one day."

After more than five decades, Dickey remains the only four-time all-conference player for N.C. State and is just one of three three-time All-Americans.

> ## "I had a fair amount of ability. Heck, I don't know if I could make the team now, but at the time I was pretty good and I played defense."
>
> [DICK DICKEY]

"I had a fair amount of ability," says Dickey, who is approaching 80 and lives in Indiana. "Heck, I don't know if I could make the team now, but at the time I was pretty good and I played defense."

And Dickey played the game the way few did at the time, making him one of the more special players in the program's history.

"I can still see that little guy. I can see his facial expressions and his haircut," said Francis of the ACC. "He was some flashy player."

VIC
MOLODET

Voters for the ACC's 50th anniversary basketball team had a tough task. The league has produced some of the most sensational players from some of the top teams in NCAA history.

Who was the best big man ever? How about the most athletic or the most competitive?

And the league's best guards? That's a hard one.

Phil Ford's name makes about every list, but who would most pick to join him in the backcourt of an ACC Dream Team? It's an argument that would include the most famous guards in league history—Duke's Bobby Hurley or Jason Williams or Johnny Dawkins, Georgia Tech's Mark Price or Kenny Anderson, Wake Forest's Tyrone Muggsy Bogues or North Carolina's Kenny Smith.

But years after Everett Case made the ACC into the super conference it would eventually become, few might come up with the name of one of the Old Gray Fox's greatest guards, Vic Molodet. His exploits have faded a bit in the yellowed pages of history, as fewer and fewer people remember just how difficult it was to break the Wolfpack's hold on winning conference tournaments back in Case's early days in Raleigh.

Maybe it's because Molodet wasn't considered the best player on the Wolfpack teams that won the first three ACC Championships from 1954 through '56. The five-foot-11 point guard often took a backseat to top scorer and rebounder Ronnie Shavlik, a mountain man who towered over teammates and opponents in those days.

VIC MOLODET

Born: February 23, 1933 (East Chicago, Indiana)
Position: Guard
High School: Washington High School, East Chicago, Indiana
Number: 73 (honored)
Years with the Wolfpack: 1954-56
NCAA Tournament Appearances: 1954 and '56
Championships: 1954, '55, '56 ACC champions; 1954, '55, '56 Dixie Classic champions
Honors:
★ Owns school record for most consecutive free throws in a game (16)
★ 1956 Everett Case Award winner (ACC Tournament Most Valuable Player)
★ 1956 First-team All-ACC selection
★ 1956 NBA eighth-round draft pick (Boston Celtics)
★ 1954, '55 Second-team All-ACC selection
★ 1956 First-team All-ACC Tournament
★ 1955 Second-team All-ACC Tournament
★ 2002 Inductee into the North Carolina Sports Hall of Fame

It's been more than 50 years since Molodet slashed and dashed his way to the basket for the Wolfpack, hurting his chances in any modern-day debate.

"Any time you're playing with a great player, one gets a little more credit than the other," says Irwin Smallwood, the longtime sports editor of the *Greensboro News & Record*, who is in the North Carolina Sports Hall of Fame with Molodet.

"I am an unabashed fan of his. When I get into arguments with younger guys talking about backcourt guys I tell them, 'Give me Molodet and you can have anybody else but Phil Ford.' Give me the two of them, and I'll beat everybody."

> # "I loved North Carolina. I wanted to get away from the big steel industry and the oil. The weather was just so pleasant. It was summer all the time. Back home, they were all freezing. I used to laugh at that."
>
> [VIC MOLODET]

Molodet, of East Chicago, Indiana, was one of a host of Hoosier prep stars Case lured to Raleigh to build his budding national power. Gary's Sammy Ranzino, Case's first All-America player and an original "Hoosier Hotshot," was among the first to make that well-worn trip between Indiana and North Carolina.

"When I was in high school I used to listen to N.C. State on the radio," Molodet says. "They would always say, 'Ranzino just steps over the 10-second line and lets it fly. Ladies and gentlemen, there it goes.' I said, 'I want to do that.' It was amazing to hear."

But N.C. State was far from a lock for Molodet, who got major recruiting attention from Illinois and many of the other schools in the Big Ten in the early 1950s. Molodet didn't decide on the Wolfpack until late in the process.

Once he got to Raleigh he never had second thoughts about leaving the Midwest and the small Indiana town Standard Oil helped build.

"I loved North Carolina," Molodet says. "I wanted to get away from the big steel industry and the oil. The weather was just so pleasant. It was summer all the time. Back home, they were all freezing. I used to laugh at that."

Molodet developed a name for himself at Washington High School with the fearless way he attacked the basket and with his variety of shots.

"That's what I needed to develop because of my size," he says. "I had my set shot, I had my jump shot, I had my drive, a stop-and-go. I had a few good shots."

And then there was the unusual shot for a player under six feet—the hook shot.

"For a guy my size, I had a deadly hook," Molodet says. "That's the truth. Anywhere around the circle I was really effective, either left or right. You see, in high school they set me up underneath and wanted me to go one on one and that's where I developed my hook shots."

Molodet, who wore No. 73 in college, didn't have much of a shot at all in his first season at State in 1954, making just 29 percent of his 609 attempts. Some wondered if Case had missed the boat on one of his Indiana prep stars.

Molodet's erratic play didn't last long, though, as Case molded the guard into more of a playmaker in the next two seasons. His shooting percentage went up to 41 percent in 1955 as he won All-ACC honors.

"It was hard to get into the groove that first season and I just had a work a little harder," Molodet says. "That's one thing I used to do was work constantly, and it paid off."

Molodet's best season came in his senior year, as he averaged 18.2 points as the Wolfpack raced up the polls to No. 2 and dreamed of a national title.

High-powered N.C. State scored 90 or more points 10 times that season and headed into the ACC Tournament with a 21-3 record and the previous two tourney titles already under its belt.

The diminutive Molodet put on a one-man show in Raleigh in the first week of March, scoring 21, 26 and 32 points en route to a third straight ACC crown. He finished 27 for 41 from the field and 25 of 29 from the foul line in the three games to win MVP honors.

It was on to the NCAA Tournament at Madison Square Garden where Molodet and the Wolfpack had their eyes fixed on a potential meeting with powerhouse San Francisco and superstar Bill Russell.

That opportunity never came as N.C. State was stunned in the opening round of the postseason in four overtimes by a little-known school named Canisius.

"That was a great basketball team and it was a shame," Smallwood says of the Wolfpack club of 1956. "It was one of those classic cases that nobody knew who Canisius was. Canisius was like the Gonzaga of today."

Molodet was called for three early charging fouls in the NCAA opener and never was much of a factor, fouling out before any of the overtime periods.

Russell and the Dons went on to win the NCAA title and North Carolina won it a season later, beating Kansas and Wilt Chamberlain.

The astonishing loss still bothers Molodet, who remembers the name of the game official who called the fouls on him as clearly as Chris Corchiani-era fans remember the name Rick Hartsell.

"That was a nightmare, that ball game," Molodet says. "If that official was here today, I believe I would kill him. He gave us a raw deal. It was a badly officiated ball game. I don't think I played two or three minutes of that game. Those three charging fouls were ridiculous.

"I can't get over that ball game, I really can't."

Molodet did get a shot at pro ball after being drafted by the Boston Celtics in the ninth round. But he didn't stick around long for one of the NBA's more storied franchises.

"There were very few small men back then," Molodet says about his short stint in the pros. "But I had a great opportunity to practice with Bob Cousy, Bill Sharmen and all the boys. That was quite an experience. I had some good times up there.

"Those guys were big back then. You look at Cousey and say he was small. Cousey wasn't small, he was about 6-1 or 6-2."

Almost five decades later, Molodet, who eventually settled in Asheville, North Carolina, still holds the N.C. State record

Courtesy of N.C. State Sports Information

with 16 straight free throws in a game, set against Wake Forest in 1956.

"That record is something I'll never forget," Molodet says. "But by today's standards that's a spit in the bucket."

Molodet's legacy at N.C. State remains one of a fiery competitor who was one of the more difficult players in the league to guard. He finished with a scoring average of 15.0 points and shot 73.5 percent from the foul line in 94 career games.

"Molodet was a streak, an absolute blazer," says ACC broadcaster and former Duke coach Bucky Waters. "He could make things happen."

Smallwood goes a step further.

"This guy would eat the lunch of a lot of these guys today who are touted as extraordinary point guards," Smallwood says. "He knew how to play north and south. He knew where the basket was. He knew that the game hinged on how many times the ball went in the basket and he knew how to get to it.

"He's got to be one of the top five guards in ACC history. It's hard to compare eras because guys now are better conditioned and they have weight training. But if he came along today he would have been the premier backcourt man playing. He probably never did get the credit he deserved because his teams never made it to the Final Four."

RONNIE
SHAVLIK

The young basketball star was being tugged by each point of the Triangle. At one time, he was ranked the most promising player in the country, a designation that might have fallen on his grandfather if anybody other than college assistants and backroom gamblers had cared to rank high school basketball prospects back then the way they are today.

But the memory of his late grandfather, a rail-thin, agile peak from the Rocky Mountains, hung heavy when it came time for this rising star to pick between the best of all basketball worlds.

"Do you think Granddaddy Big Man"—that's what all the grandkids call the grandfather none of them had ever met—"would be upset if I didn't go to State?" he asked. The young man knew much of his grandfather's exploits, having seen his name countless times while watching ACC basketball games as a kid.

Beverly Shavlik smiled and answered quickly, looking into the eyes of her late husband, but talking to her six-foot-10 grandson.

"Indeed he would not be," she said. "He wants you to make your own decision. He wants you to be yourself. This is your life. He would be the first to tell you if he were sitting right here: You make your own name, but whatever you do, do it well and do it graciously."

There is so much of Ronnie Shavlik in Shavlik Randolph that sometimes Beverly has to do a double take when her grandson walks in the room. From the way he folds up his dirty gym socks to the way he answers a stranger in his deep, polite big man's voice, there are things that make her return to her

RONNIE SHAVLIK

Born: December 4, 1933 (Denver, Colorado)
Died: June 27, 1983, of pancreatic cancer
High School: Denver East High School, Denver, Colorado.
Position: Center
Number: 84 (honored)
Years with the Wolfpack: 1954-56
NCAA Tournament Appearances: 1954 and '56
Championships: 1954, '55 and '56 ACC champions; 1954, '55, '56 Dixie Classic champions.
Honors:
★ Owns school record with 1,598 career rebounds
★ Led ACC in rebounding in 1956 at 19.5 rebounds per game, highest rebounding average in conference history
★ 1954, '55 Dixie Classic Most Valuable Player
★ 1955, '56 First-team All-America
★ 1955, '56 First-team All-ACC selection
★ 1954, '55 First-team All-ACC Tournament
★ 1956 ACC Player of the Year
★ 1956 Second-team All-ACC Tournament
★ 1955 Everett Case Winner (Most Valuable Player of the ACC Tournament)
★ 1956 Alumni Athletic Trophy winner
★ 1956 NBA first-round pick (New York Knicks, fourth overall)
★ Member of the ACC 50th Anniversary team
★ Founder, Wake County Shelter Workshop, 1954
★ Named 1963 Employer of the Year for employing handicapped workers
★ Awarded 1965 Presidential Meritorious Award by President Lyndon B. Johnson for employing handicapped workers
★ 1979 Inductee into the North Carolina Sports Hall of Fame
★ 1980 NCAA Silver Anniversary Award Winner
★ President and Vice President of the NCSU Student Aid Association

courtship with Ronnie, whom she met when he was a sophomore basketball star at N.C. State.

"It's like Ronnie is standing there with me," she says.

"He has to be awfully damned good to be able to accomplish this against college players and guys who were ready to go to the pros."

[VIC BUBAS]

But Ronnie Shavlik died five months before Shavlik Randolph was born. That hasn't prevented the young prodigy from keeping Shavlik's name alive, even though he opted to attend rival Duke University and play for Mike Krzyzewski instead of N.C. State or North Carolina, where his parents met. Some two decades after his grandfather's death, Shavlik Randolph revived interest in the career of the Atlantic Coast Conference's first true superstar, a lanky but dominating post player who wore jersey No. 84, by declaring that he wore No. 42 in the hopes that he would one day be half as good as his late grandfather.

There was no reason, in 1952, for Ronald Dean Shavlik to come east from Denver, Colorado, to Raleigh, North Carolina, other than he wanted to make his own way in life. The grandson of Czechoslovakian immigrants, his family had put tenuous roots on the side of the Rockies and he expected he would settle there as well. The thing was, he became a terrific basketball player.

His parents didn't particularly approve of his choice of a pastime, but Ronnie kept growing and getting better at the game, which he learned by playing with his buddies on the streets of Denver's Park Hill area.

When they were old enough to start playing organized ball, they called themselves "The Educated Five," an early glance into what Ronnie Shavlik thought was most important about the game of basketball. It was a means to getting an education that would eventually turn him into one of the most respected businessmen and civic leaders Raleigh ever had.

Young Ronnie started as a sophomore at Denver's East High School and led the Angels to a pair of Colorado state championships as a junior and senior. But he really caught the eye of college recruiters—especially former Wolfpack assistant Vic Bubas—following his performance in the national AAU Tournament, which was held in Denver in 1952.

Bubas read in a Chicago newspaper account of a 17-year-old high school player on the unseeded Jessel Electrics team, a local champion of the YMCA leagues that had been invited to represent the host city in the nationally prominent event. Shavlik played so well against bigger, older, more experienced competition that he was named the tournament's Most Promising Player.

"He has to be awfully damned good to be able to accomplish this against college players and guys who were ready to go to the pros," Bubas told Case. "Maybe this kid is worth a look."

"Oh, we're never going to get anybody from Denver," Case responded. "I don't even know anybody in Denver."

"Well, we won't get him if we don't try," Bubas said.

Others tried awfully hard as well. Shavlik had caught the eye of Case's mortal enemy, Kentucky coach Adolph Rupp, as well as UCLA's John Wooden, Oklahoma A&M's Hank Iba and the other big-name coaches of the day.

But after taking recruiting trips back East, and seeing all points of the country during his chauffeured wooing, Shavlik chose to play for Case.

"I hadn't really seen much of the South," Shavlik told George Benedict of the Wolfpacker in 1981. "I came down here and was impressed with the area. I also wanted to get away and do something on my own. It was nice here, there were a lot of ambitious ideas about the basketball program, and the people at State were top notch."

Nevertheless, rumors were circulated by a loser in the recruiting sweepstakes about excessive benefits that Shavlik would receive for playing for the Wolfpack, including three airline tickets home every year, a membership at a Raleigh country club and a set of golf clubs. The NCAA investigated, found the rumors to be unfounded, but discovered enough recruiting violations in trying out more than a dozen other prospective players that it placed the Wolfpack on a one-year probation. Thus, State was ineligible to play in the NCAA Tournament in Shavlik's sophomore year.

Shavlik quickly became a star in the newly formed ACC, running the court, fighting for rebounds and scoring at will against smaller opponents. He was a big man who could run, able to keep up with the M-Twins,

John Maglio and Vic Molodet. And his hook shot was unstoppable.

"He was the main man on those teams," said Molodet, who shared All-America honors with Shavlik as a senior. "For his size, that boy moved up and down the court pretty well. He was always around the hole. He was always where the ball was. When you can pick up 22, 23 rebounds a game, that's pretty damned good, isn't it?"

Indeed, Shavlik still owns the N.C. State rebounding record with an astounding 1,598, which is 552 more boards than second-place Tommy Burleson and second all time in the ACC. He owns 13 of the top 14 rebounding games in school history and is ranked one, two and three for the school's top rebounding seasons with 472, 581 and 545 in his three seasons with the Wolfpack.

Shavlik's other personal and team accomplishments are amazing: he led the Wolfpack to the ACC Championship in each of his three seasons of varsity play. Against Villanova as a senior, he had 49 points and 35 rebounds. He was the ACC Tournament's MVP in 1955 and the ACC Player of the Year in 1956, and first-team All-ACC both years. He's the only player in the history of the Dixie Classic to be named MVP twice.

But, in then end, his career ended with the ultimate disappointment: an unexpected loss in the NCAA Tournament.

The 1956 Wolfpack was probably Case's most talented and accomplished team. It beat fifth-ranked Brigham Young and cruised past a Dixie Classic field that included two other Top 10 teams. Three losses in ACC play did not diminish the Wolfpack nationally, and it ended the regular season ranked second in the Associated Press poll behind Bill Russell and San Francisco. It appeared that Case, the man who won so many high school championships in Indiana, would finally get a chance to win a national championship on the college level.

But in the regular-season finale against Wake Forest, Shavlik broke his wrist and was thought to be lost for the season. A Raleigh doctor made a special leather lace-up cast for Shavlik, and he managed to return for the ACC Tournament and help the Wolfpack win its third consecutive league championship.

The first step in the NCAA Tournament was lightly regarded Canisius, of Buffalo, New York. The Wolfpack players had their eyes on a championship matchup with Russell and the rest of the San Francisco Dons.

Shavlik, whose celebrity for playing hurt in the ACC Tournament earned him a guest appearance on the *Perry Como Show* that week, was terrific for a one-handed rebounder, scoring 25 points and grabbing 17 rebounds. But his teammates weren't sharp, and Canisius pushed the Wolfpack to four overtimes in Madison Square Garden. After John Maglio missed a free throw with 14 seconds to play, a little-used reserve named Frank Corcoran scored his only basket of the game and ended Shavlik's All-America career. Case called it "my greatest disappointment in 36 years in basketball."

But Shavlik's career, and life, were hardly defined by his basketball career. The game was a means of getting an education, and it never consumed him.

"Basketball was a big part of my life, but there comes a day when you can't eat that basketball," Shavlik once told Bruce Phillips of the *Raleigh Times*. "You have to have something else."

So even after he was drafted as the fourth pick in the 1956 NBA draft by the New York Knicks, Shavlik was also trying to develop a small janitorial company he and Beverly started in his last year of school. It was a simple concept, really, one he brought with him after spending a summer on the maintenance staff of a Denver racetrack. He simply got contracts to clean office buildings in and around Cameron Village, where he and Beverly lived in an apartment not far from Case's house.

Eventually, those contracts were more valuable than the one he signed with the Knicks, which was worth $14,000 a year with a $5,000 signing bonus. Plus, his heart just wasn't in the NBA.

"I didn't have much enthusiasm for pro ball," Shavlik told former N.C. State sports information director Ed Seaman, when the latter worked at the *Fayetteville Observer*. "The adjustment was too big. They expected more than I was ready to give. As a result, they lost confidence in me, and I did in myself."

He played only two years in the NBA, and spent three more seasons moonlighting with the Baltimore Bullets in the old Eastern League. Eventually, he just stopped playing and concentrated on his janitorial business, which eventually grew to three separate companies, worth as much as $250 million and covering 40 states.

"Basketball was fun for him, but it was just a game," Beverly Shavlik says. "It was a game for him. You are disappointed when you lose, but it is not a tragedy or a travesty. That's how he felt about basketball."

"He was big in every way,
except in the head."

[LEE TERRILL]

Shavlik began his lifelong outreach to those less fortunate than he while in school, as a Big Brother to an eight-year-old boy. He was also encouraged by Case to spend time at the Governor Morehead School for the Blind, which is across the street from the N.C. State campus. Eventually, Shavlik became one of the state's largest employers of the handicapped. In 1965, he was given the Meritorious Award by president Lyndon Johnson.

Shavlik accepted many honors and awards throughout his life of civic service, and in 1979 he was inducted into the North Carolina Sports Hall of Fame. One of the awards he was most proud of was the 1980 NCAA Silver Anniversary Award, which is presented annually to five former athletes who have been successful after their college careers were over. Shavlik and former Virginia standout Wally Walker are the only two ACC basketball players to ever win the award.

In 1983, about the time the Wolfpack began its miraculous run for the school's second NCAA championship, Shavlik was diagnosed with pancreatic cancer. He struggled to follow the Wolfpack from Raleigh to Atlanta for the ACC Tournament, then made the draining trip to Albuquerque, New Mexico, for the Final Four. In between State's win over Georgia in the semifinals and its upset of Houston in the title game, Shavlik took his family on one last car ride through the southern part of the Rocky Mountains.

"He was very mad that he had cancer," Beverly Shavlik said. "It's the first time I ever really saw him display that side of him in 27 years of marriage."

But on the morning of the title game, a light snow fell outside Shavlik's hotel room. Several Wolfpack players and head coach Jim Valvano came by his room to visit before they headed over to The Pit for the game. Shavlik, who at the time was the president of the Wolfpack Club, knew that it would probably be the last N.C. State game he ever saw.

"He was thrilled," Beverly Shavlik said of State's last-second victory over the Cougars. "It could not have ended any better than that."

Shavlik died on June 27, 1983, long before Shavlik Randolph became a hot basketball prospect, or before his jersey was honored by N.C. State, or before a couple of his childhood friends pushed to get him inducted into the Colorado Sports Hall of Fame, which finally happened in 2001.

Former Wolfpack assistant coach Lee Terrill best summed up Shavlik's basketball and career in news accounts of his death.

"He was big in every way," Terrill said, "except in the head."

DIXIE
BASKETBALL
CLASSIC
1954

MOST VALUABLE
PLAYER

LOU
PUCILLO

How on earth could a nun tell such a lie? That's what Lou Pucillo wondered when he graduated from Southeast Catholic High School in 1955. A few years before, the nuns at St. Monica School in Philadelphia told the eighth-graders that if they made a novena, a promise to go to church nine straight days, all their dreams would come true.

Pucillo, who gave up the church choir to devote all his spare time to playing basketball, had asked for something relatively simple. All he wanted to do was play basketball at a major university, just like his idol Bob Cousy.

Trouble was, Pucillo never grew into his dreams. By the time he graduated high school, he was only five foot nine, 157 pounds and did not expect to get any bigger. He had been cut from Southeast's basketball teams as a freshman and a sophomore. He didn't even try out for the team as a junior, figuring that the coach would cut him again. So he stuck to pickup games and both the CYO and PAL leagues.

After all, Southeast's coach was pretty knowledgeable. His name was Jack Kraft, and in 1971 he took Villanova's basketball team to the NCAA championship game against UCLA.

But Kraft used Pucillo sparingly during his senior season. The small point guard never started a game and averaged a little over four points per outing. The frustrated point guard rarely got to show off his slick passing skills or his exaggerated jumpshot that he so often lofted over taller opponents. Pucillo never felt like such a failure as he did on the night of his senior athletics banquet, as his

career officially came to an end without any college recruiters knocking on his door.

So Pucillo followed his father's wishes and enrolled at Temple Prep School, where the elder Pucillo was a foreign language teacher, the summer after his graduation, hoping to take a couple of Spanish courses in case he ever got the chance to go to college. To the younger Pucillo's surprise, Temple had a basketball team that seemed to be pretty decent. He opted to enroll for the fall

"He shows me something different every time I see him play. He's always thinking one step ahead of everyone else on the court."

[EVERETT CASE]

and winter quarters, just for the opportunity to play on another basketball team.

Little did he know that the nuns of St. Monica might have actually been telling the truth.

Pucillo averaged more than 25 points a game for Temple, helping the team to a near-perfect 25-1 record. One afternoon, as Pucillo played lackadaisically against the Philadelphia School for the Blind and Deaf, Vic Bubas, one of Everett Case's assistants at N.C. State, happened to be in the stands scouting Philadelphia talent. The Wolfpack had already signed six-foot-nine Philadelphia schoolboy legend John Richter to play for Case, and was looking for more Philly boys to flush out the roster.

Bubas liked what he saw in Pucillo, even though his style was the antithesis of Case's basic coaching philosophy. The Old Gray Fox liked big guards who were disciplined and always in control. Pucillo was about as tightly reined as a tornado. He was an unabashed hot dog, a style that perfectly matched his gregarious personality. He loved making difficult behind-the-back and between-the-legs passes to streaking teammates on the fast break.

Bubas called back to Raleigh to report what he had seen that day and how excited he was about the diminutive guard, who made outlandish passes and bounced the ball between his legs the way that dribbling fool, Cousy, had done when the Wolfpack beat Holy Cross in the 1950 NCAA Tournament.

When Bubas suggested that Case completely change his coaching style and offer this Pucillo kid a scholarship, there was a long pause on the other end of the line.

"Vic," Case asked, "have you been drinking?"

Bubas was perfectly sober, and he invited Pucillo to visit the campus in Raleigh. Pucillo quickly signed when Case made him a scholarship offer, since no other school in the country had been willing to take that chance. He was the smallest player Case ever signed to a scholarship at N.C. State.

Pucillo eventually won over his old coach, with a style that led *Raleigh Times* sportswriter Bruce Phillips to call him a "hardwood Houdini." In fact, Pucillo became one of Case's favorite players.

"He shows me something different every time I see him play," Case once said of Pucillo. "He's always thinking one step ahead of everyone else on the court."

Pucillo got his first chance to show his coach something in the 1956 Dixie Classic. The Wolfpack was struggling against Iowa in the first round of the event, and Case decided to shake up his lineup going into the second half. Pucillo sparked his team to an 84-70 whipping of the unranked Hawkeyes.

Two years later, Pucillo led the Wolfpack on one of its most brilliant stretches, when the Wolfpack on three consecutive days beat Louisville in overtime, second-ranked Cincinnati with Oscar Robertson and seventh-ranked Michigan State with Jumping Johnny Green in the 1958 Dixie Classic.

Because of a four-year NCAA probation, the Wolfpack was not allowed to compete in the NCAA Tournament that year, but Pucillo and Richter helped Case have one of his finest teams ever at N.C. State. The duo made an odd basketball couple, as was profiled in a 1959 issue of *Life* magazine.

"A perennial basketball giant, North Carolina State has come up with the season's oddest and best set of co-stars," the story began. "One of them, five-foot-nine Lou Pucillo, looks like a scrawny mismate for the other, John Richter, who stands at a model basketball height of six feet, eight inches."

Pucillo scored 22 points in the Wolfpack's win over Michigan State, then ended his career with 23 points in the ACC Championship game against a heavily favored North Carolina team, a victory that gave Case his 10th and final conference championship.

At season's end, both Pucillo and Richter were named first-team All-Americans. Pucillo, who never thought he would end up playing college basketball after his years of frustration in high school, won every possible award following his final season: ACC Tournament Most Valuable Player,

ACC Player of the Year, ACC Athlete of the Year and the N.C. State Alumni Athletic Trophy.

While Richter went on to become a first-round draft pick of the Boston Celtics and won an NBA Championship in his only year in the league, Pucillo only played a smattering of professional basketball, where he indeed was too small to play with the rest of the giants.

But neither Bubas nor Case ever saw a better ball handler in the days of coaching. It was only natural that he follow in their footsteps of teaching the game. Pucillo was all set to become the head coach at Greensboro's Page High School in 1951, when Case called on him to replace assistant coach Lee Terrill on the Wolfpack bench. Pucillo got out of his contract with the Greensboro City Schools to join Case as the Wolfpack's freshman coach.

Pucillo stayed there for three years before going to work for a friend of Case's in the liquor distribution business. He eventually owned his own beverage brokerage company, a business he sold when he retired in 2001.

There may have been smaller guards to play at N.C. State—such as five-foot-five Monte Towe and five-foot-seven Spud Webb—but even those Mighty Mites weren't as big a gamble as Pucillo was for Case back in the mid-1950s.

"He is walking proof that there is still room for the little man in college basketball—if, as Lou was, you are willing to pay the price of practice," Case once told Irwin Smallwood of the *Greensboro Daily News*.

Hank Walker/Time Life Pictures/Getty Images

But Pucillo also believes that it was more than just hard work that brought him from Philadelphia to Raleigh, where he became an all-star and a successful businessman.

"I am a big believer in destiny," said Pucillo, who has been inducted into both the North Carolina and Pennsylvania Halls of Fame. "The odds of me ever playing big-time college basketball and getting some regional and national awards were crazy. You don't just not play high school basketball and score just four points a game, and then have one scout see you against a deaf-and-mute team, if there wasn't some kind of reason somewhere. You can call it spiritual, or whatever you want to call it. But it happened."

Maybe those nuns weren't lying after all.

EDDIE BIEDENBACH

Sitting on the front steps at Reynolds Coliseum that Monday morning, Eddie Biedenbach was trying to figure out what he was going to tell his dad. How could he go back to Pittsburgh and tell Big Ed that he had been kicked off the team, that he had lost his scholarship at N.C. State, that he had back-talked one of the greatest coaches in college basketball history?

"All I could think was that my dad was going to kill me when I got home," Biedenbach says.

Biedenbach was no rebel, but he was a wild and undisciplined player when he arrived in Raleigh, so much so that Case affectionately called him "Wildhorse."

Well, two days before, Biedenbach was in the starting line up in a scrimmage game against the Citadel, mainly because regular starter Tommy Maddocks was late for practice.

At one point, Biedenbach stole the ball from a Citadel player and raced in for a layup, but Case didn't say anything to him. A few minutes later, the same player stole the ball from Biedenbach and went in for an easy layup. Case called timeout and quickly put the late-arriving Maddocks into the lineup.

"He started cussing me," Biedenbach remembers. "I said, 'But, Coach...'"

That was a mistake. Case didn't like to be challenged, a trait he passed on to Norm Sloan years before.

"You get your ass out of here, and don't you ever come back," Case yelled at the sophomore guard on that afternoon in Reynolds Coliseum.

EDDIE BIEDENBACH

Born: August 12, 1945 (Pittsburgh, Pennsylvania)
High School: Edgewood High School, Edgewood, Pennsylvania
Degree: B.S. in Forest Resources, N.C. State, 1968
Position: Guard, assistant coach
Number: 34
Years with the Wolfpack: 1965-68 (player), 1969-78, 1993-96 (assistant coach).
NCAA Tournament Appearances: 1965, '73, '74, 2003
Championships: 1965, '73, '74 ACC
Championships: 1974 NCAA Championship; 1981 Southern Conference regular-season championship; 1998 Big South regular-season championship, 2003 Big South Tournament Championship.
Honors:
★ 1966, '68 First-team All-ACC selection
★ 1966, '68 First-team All-ACC Tournament
★ 1967 NBA ninth-round draft pick (St. Louis Hawks, 89th overall pick)
★ 1968 NBA fourth-round draft pick (Los Angeles Lakers, 45th overall pick)
★ 1998, 2002 Big South Coach of the Year
★ 1998 Inductee into the East Boros (Pennsylvania) Hall of Fame

"I thought he meant forever," Biedenbach says. "I went down in the locker room and cleaned out my locker. All I could think was 'Boy, Big Ed is going to kill me.'"

Two days later, Biedenbach was making his arrangements to go back to Pittsburgh, but he wanted to apologize to the coach. So he waited for the big purple Cadillac to pull into the parking lot at Reynolds that morning.

"Wildhorse, how you doing?" Case said as he walked to his office.

"Coach, I just want to apologize for talking back to you," Biedenbach said.

"Those guys taught me if you play hard, if you listen and try to play together, you can be a good player. They taught me to understand the game better."

[EDDIE BIEDENBACH]

"Aren't you supposed to be in class?"

"Yes, sir, I have an eight o'clock class, and I am due there in a few minutes."

"Then get your ass to class."

Case had either forgotten about the altercation or, more likely, he just moved on.

"He was just trying to make a point and I learned it quickly," Biedenbach says.

It was one of the few lessons Biedenbach was able to learn from the Old Gray Fox, who resigned two games into Biedenbach's first year on the Wolfpack varsity.

But that's one of the reasons that Biedenbach is such a vital link in the history of N.C. State basketball. He played for Case, Press Maravich and Norm Sloan. As an assistant, he recruited Tommy Burleson, David Thompson and Kenny Carr. He was on the opposite sidelines in 1983, when the Wolfpack beat Georgia at The Pit in Albuquerque, New Mexico, in the NCAA semifinals. And he returned to Raleigh later in his career, both as an assistant to Les Robinson and again as a head coach at UNC-Asheville.

Don't take this the wrong way, but in many ways, Biedenbach is the Forest Gump of N.C. State basketball, someone who has

been on hand for many of the greatest moments in the program's history. He could probably fill a volume by himself.

When he came to Raleigh for Case's basketball camp at the North Carolina State Fairgrounds, Biedenbach was little more than a talented athlete with few basketball skills. He was feisty and reckless. But working with Lou Pucillo on the freshman team, then Case, Maravich and Sloan on the varsity, Biedenbach became an accomplished player who was twice named first-team All-ACC.

"Those guys taught me if you play hard, if you listen and try to play together, you can be a good player," Biedenbach says. "They taught me to understand the game better. It wasn't anything astounding, they just worked hard at teaching me the mental and physical fundamentals of the game."

The highlight of Biedenbach's playing career came early, when he helped the Wolfpack win its unexpected 1965 championship as a sophomore, with an ailing Case on the sidelines watching.

Biedenbach still gets goose bumps when thinking about walking up the 23 steps from the locker room to the main floor at Reynolds before that game, and entering the smoke-filled arena. He also remembers in the final moments of that game being fouled by a Duke player and being grabbed from behind by someone on the baseline under the basket.

Biedenbach gave his assailant a good, swift elbow to the ribs, only to turn around and discover it was Maravich, who was giving his player a hug from behind for creating a good play. (In those days, team benches were underneath the baskets.)

But by playing so hard, Biedenbach also suffered a string of injuries. Heading into his senior season, he suffered a back injury that required surgery and forced him to sit out as a medical redshirt during Sloan's first season as head coach.

He came back from the back injury to lead the 1967-68 team with a 14.1 scoring average and earned first-team all-conference honors for the second time. He even led the Wolfpack back to the ACC title game, thanks to one of the more controversial games in tournament history: the 12-10 game against Duke.

All most people remember about that game was the incredibly long stretches with nothing more than senior center Bill Kretzer dribbling the ball near midcourt. But Biedenbach will never forget a conversation he had with Sloan on the sidelines with three minutes to play.

Sloan called Biedenbach over, and Duke guard Tony Barone went with him.

"Eddie, with two and a half minutes to go, I want you to just take the ball and make something happen," Sloan said.

"Don't you want me to call a time out so we can set up a play?" Beidenbach said,

motioning with his head that Barone was standing right there listening to the strategy.

"No, you dumb so-and-so, if we call a time out they will take the midget out and put in someone who can guard you," Sloan answered.

Biedenbach hit an 18-foot jumper with 2:29 on the clock, tying the game 8-8, and the Wolfpack went on to beat the sixth-ranked Blue Devils by the famous score of 12-10.

"He loved the game of basketball," says Vann Williford, who was a teammate for Biedenbach's for one season. "He was the best defensive player I can ever remember. He was never out of shape. We were always running suicides and sprints and things, and one time we had this doctor there taking some measurements and readings of our heart rate before exercise and after exercise.

"At the end of the exercise, everybody else's heart rate was over 100. Eddie's was 45 at rest and 55 after sprints. He was just a freak."

After a brief attempt at a pro career, Biedenbach returned to N.C. State to become an assistant for Sloan and perhaps make his greatest contribution to the Wolfpack program.

First, he helped with the recruitment of 7-4 center Tommy Burleson, mainly by driving to the mountains and maintaining the relationship Sloan had already established with the big man.

But it was also in recruiting Burleson that he learned of Thompson. While watching a playoff game between Burleson's Newland High and Marion High School, an N.C. State fan introduced Thompson to Biedenbach and told him that this junior player had been the conference Most Valuable Player, beating out seniors like Burleson.

Biedenbach didn't actually see Thompson play until the following Christmas, when he went to Kings Mountain to watch another player. He stopped by Shelby's Crest High School and watched some film. He liked the way Thompson jumped, but initially wasn't that impressed with his shooting skills.

But the first time he saw Thompson in person, his eyes popped out of the gym.

"He comes out to warm up, and I saw that he was unusually strong and a strong jumping kid," Biedenbach says. "The game started and he made the first three shots, and he had three guys guarding him. I never knew if he could shoot a jumper or not, because no matter who was guarding him, he laid it in. At halftime, I ran to the locker room and called Coach Sloan. "Coach, I don't know who you know in Shelby, but whoever it is, we have to call him. This is the best guy I have ever seen.'

"I had played with Jerry West and against Oscar Robertson. David was as good as I had ever seen and he was just 16 years old. We started recruiting him right then."

Initially, Thompson seemed to be a lock for North Carolina. He had attended Dean Smith's camp the summer before his senior season, while the Wolfpack was pursuing Ray Harrison, a small forward from Greensboro's Page High School, who had attended Sloan camp at N.C. State.

But Biedenbach, who had just gotten married in the spring of 1970, continued his dogged pursuit of Thompson in Shelby.

Smith, the retired Tar Heel coach, remembered feeling good about the prospect of signing Thompson.

"Then I went to be the speaker at the Crest sports banquet that spring, and I looked out in the crowd and saw Eddie Biedenbach," Smith says. "I thought 'Uh oh.'"

Sure enough, one morning Biedenbach gave Thompson a ride to school, and Thompson chose that day to tell the assistant coach that he was ready to sign a national letter of intent.

The only problem was, Biedenbach didn't have a copy of the official contract for Thompson to sign. The two got back in his car—despite Thompson's protests that he would be late for school—in search of a letter to sign. Biedenbach found one at his hotel, then raced to the family's home to get the signature of Thompson's father, Vellie.

With that, Biedenbach secured the greatest player in the history of the Atlantic Coast Conference.

"My wife has often said that I spent more time with David Thompson than I did with her that first year we were married," says Biedenbach, who has had head coaching jobs at Davidson and UNC-Asheville. "I always tell her, 'Well, he was a better player.' She's never really appreciated that."

But Wolfpack fans who marveled at Thompson's great talent and leaping ability certainly as he, Burleson and Monte Towe led the Wolfpack to its first NCAA championship certainly appreciated the investment of time and the contributions Biedenbach made to the school's basketball tradition.

NORM
SLOAN

R arely has a nickname ever fit more perfectly than Stormin' Norman Sloan, and rarely has one ever been more despised by its owner.

"You only call me that because it rhymes," Sloan told the worms who used that nickname, which he loathed like a mustard stain on one of his plaid jackets.

Apparently, he had never seen himself standing rigid on the sidelines, his hands trembling with intense anticipation of the competition ahead, as his wife Joan sang the national anthem. He never saw himself stomping on the sidelines, berating his players for not doing things his way or an official for not calling things his way.

Later in life, he finally admitted what everyone already knew.

"I deserved it," he said of the nickname.

Sloan could be a snapping turtle, unwilling to let something go until he heard the distant rumble of thunder. Once, while in his second stint as the head coach at Florida, Sloan was a little upset at the way Georgia fans were hurling debris at him and his players. He went after the campus policeman who was in charge of protecting the Gators as they left the court and told him: "You're a gutless little fucker, aren't you?"

For the next hour and a half, the guy who was supposed to protect Sloan, stormed around Stegeman Coliseum trying to put the coach in handcuffs and haul him downtown. He might have succeeded, too, had two of Sloan's biggest players not blocked the doorway to the visiting locker room.

Sloan, an Indianapolis native who was one of Everett Case's six original "Hoosier Hotshots," loved his ties to the Old Gray Fox.

NORM SLOAN

Born: June 25, 1926 (Indianapolis, Indiana)
Died: December 9, 2003, of pulmonary fibrosis
High School: Lawrence Central High School, Indianapolis, Indiana
Degree: B.S., Education, N.C. State, 1951
Position: Guard, head coach
Number: 75
Years with the Wolfpack: 1947-49 (player), 1966-80 (coach)
Record: 627-395 in 37 years overall at Presbyterian, The Citadel, N.C. State and Florida; 266-127 in 13 seasons at N.C. State
NCAA Tournament Appearances: 1970, '74, '79, '87, '88, '89
Championships: 1970 ACC championship, '73 ACC championship, '74 ACC championship, '89 Southeastern Conference championship; 1974 NCAA championship
Honors:
★ 1957 Southern Conference Coach of the Year
★ 1970, '73, '74 ACC Coach of the Year
★ 1984 Inductee into the Indiana Basketball Hall of Fame
★ 1994 Inductee into the North Carolina Sports Hall of Fame
★ Winningest coach in University of Florida history (235-194)
★ Lettered in three sports at N.C. State (basketball, football and track)
★ Whistle honored

But, typical of Sloan, he stormed away from Case's program with a year of eligibility remaining, primarily because he got little playing time behind a star guard named Vic Bubas.

"Coach, there's only two people in the world who think Bubas is better than me: you and him," Sloan told Case.

"But, Norm, we're winning," Case shot back.

> ## "It was pure coaching genius, even though we never planned on holding the ball. It was just how things happened. In the end, Norm completely outcoached him, because he knew how stubborn Bubas was."
>
> [VANN WILLIFORD]

"Yeah, but with me, we would be winning by more," Sloan said.

So he spent his senior year not on the hardwoods with Case, but playing quarterback for football coach Beattie Feathers instead.

But Sloan absorbed plenty about basketball, so much so that when he met up with Bubas again one night in the Charlotte Coliseum, the two Case protégés faced off in a bout of stubbornness in which Sloan won in an unconventional and controversial manner. It was the 1968 ACC Tournament, and Sloan was in his second year as the head coach of his alma mater and Bubas was in his ninth year as head coach of the Blue Devils. Duke was ranked sixth in the nation and had beaten the Wolfpack handily in two regular-season meetings, thanks primarily to the inside play of Mike Lewis.

When the two teams met in the semifinals of the ACC Tournament, Sloan turned his offense inside out in hopes of forcing Bubas to bring Lewis from under the basket. So Bill Kretzer and Vann Williford started the game at the top of the offense instead of under the basket. But Bubas didn't budge.

The result was one of the weirdest games in ACC Tournament history, as Kretzer spent most of the game either holding the ball or dribbling it near midcourt, while the entire arena was practically bored to tears. But the Wolfpack won, and Sloan got the best of Bubas without stomping off to the football field.

"It was pure coaching genius, even though we never planned on holding the ball," Williford says. "It was just how things happened. In the end, Norm completely outcoached him, because he knew how stubborn Bubas was."

Two years later, the Wolfpack slowed things down against Frank McGuire and South Carolina in the championship game, and Williford helped lead State to its first of three ACC Championships under Sloan.

Those were the days when Sloan was just building his program, when he didn't have as much talent as Duke or North Carolina. That changed dramatically when Sloan landed Tommy Burleson from Newland, North Carolina, in 1970 and David Thompson of Boiling Springs, North Carolina, in 1971. They were the foundation

for one of the greatest teams in college basketball, the squad that in 1974 ended UCLA's
reign over the game.

With Burleson in the middle,
Thompson all over the court, and tiny point
guard Monte Towe running the show, the
Wolfpack won 57 of 58 games over a two-year
span and brought home the school's first basketball national championship.

"I always thought Norm was an under-
rated coach," said Lefty Driesell, the former
Maryland coach who was Sloan's adversary
on the court, but his partner in getting under
the skin of North Carolina coach Dean Smith.
"He never had McDonald's All-Americans,
but he knew how to coach and get the most
out of his players. They always competed
hard."

But Sloan also rode his charges
extremely hard. More than a handful couldn't
take it and left the program over the years.
Those who stayed, however, were defiantly
loyal to their old coach.

"Norm could be brutal," Williford says.
"But he was only brutal for the day. If you
screwed up in practice or you screwed up in a
game, you were going to hear about it in great
detail. Probably a lot of other people were
going to hear about it, too. But the next day, it
was done, unless of course you did the same
stupid thing again. There were some players
who didn't either understand that or couldn't
handle it, and it ate at them."

Sloan never lost his fiery, my-way
approach, which did not serve him well in the
two times he ended up being investigated by
the NCAA. He landed on probation both
times, for one year at N.C. State for the
recruitment of David Thompson and for two

years at Florida for buying player Vernon
Maxwell a $240 plane ticket to a Boston
Celtics basketball camp.

The latter scandal, which included a
Drug Enforcement Agency investigation into
the basketball program during his second
stint at Florida, brought about Sloan's forced
retirement on October 31, 1989. Or, as he
called it, the Halloween Day Massacre.

Sloan was firm with his players, no
question. Every year before the start of practice, he called the team together to state his
simple rules: Go to class, trim your hair, tuck
in your shirts, have your ankles taped before
practice every day and be on time.

"If you don't want to do that, then
don't worry about it," Sloan would say. "You
don't have to do any of those things. But you
have to pay your own way to college and you
can't play basketball for me."

Burleson remembers his first meeting
as a signed player for the Wolfpack. Sloan
had courted the seven-foot-four center for
nearly three years, lavishing all kind of attention on the center who would end up as the
centerpiece for a national championship.

"Now, guys, you are on campus and
you have accepted a scholarship," Sloan told
the freshmen. "The steak dinners and shrimp
cocktails have come to an end. I am going to
be demanding in practice. There will be a lot
expected of you in academics. You are going
to have to earn your scholarship now. You are
going to be role models for this program. You
are not going to go to parties and go to bars
and damage the reputation of the N.C. State
basketball program."

There was no doubt in the players'
minds that Sloan meant it.

"You never had to guess where he stood about anything," Williford says. "If you wanted to hear what he thought, all you had to do was ask."

Yet, Sloan had no problems with breaking NCAA rules if he thought a player needed help. In his book, *Confessions of a Coach*, Sloan admitted that he broke multiple rules, both as a player and coach at N.C. State and at Florida. Generally, he gave players in need money for trips home or to help their families. He helped Phil Spence's mother buy the heart medication she needed. He loaned Tommy

Burleson, who came from a poor farmer's family in the mountains of North Carolina, the $20 Burleson needed for his dorm deposit. He even helped an unnamed player and his girlfriend get an abortion. But Sloan adamantly insisted—both to the NCAA Infractions Committee that he faced on two occasions and to the public—that he didn't cheat to get a player.

"I adopted a simple precept that basically never changed," Sloan wrote. "In relation to the NCAA's ever-expanding rules, I've primarily been concerned with illegal

"My responsibility on that team, to be honest with you, was not to screw it up."

[NORM SLOAN]

aid, offered or given, as an inducement to get an athlete to attend my school. If I went out and tried to buy him, that was cheating.

"But to me, once a kid gets there, he's family, particularly if it's a kid without a family that can take care of his basic human needs. When you go in a home to recruit now, one of the of the first things the father or the mother—or both—will say is, 'I just want to make sure you will take care of my son. I want to make sure that when he has problems, there is someone he can go talk to.' That's something a coach tells the parents he will do and something I feel he should do."

As a later addition to Sloan's much-hated "Worm Brigade" (his pet name for the media), I never really saw the "Stormin'" part of Sloan's personality. He mellowed like a fine wine—OK, he calmed down like a seltzer in stomach acid—after he retired to North Carolina in 1990. One afternoon in 1999, he sat for hours at a Raleigh seafood restaurant to talk about his colorful career, bringing along his grandson to hear the retelling of the Wolfpack's "Golden Years."

Here are a few highlights from that broad-ranging interview.

• "When we came here, people in this part of the country were basketball illiterates. They didn't know anything about it, and they didn't care anything about it. Reynolds Coliseum helped create the most rabid area of

fans for basketball that there is anywhere in the country," Sloan said of his arrival as one of Case's "Hoosier Hotshots."

• "We took a bad lick. It was uncalled for, it was inexcusable, it was laughable compared to what goes on today," Sloan said of the one-year probation that kept the undefeated 1973 team out of the NCAA Tournament.

• "My responsibility on that team, to be honest with you, was not to screw it up," Sloan said of the 1974 team that won the national championship.

Sloan recruited the foundation for another national championship squad: Dereck Whittenburg, Sidney Lowe and Thurl Bailey. But by the time those three were cutting down the nets in Albuquerque, New Mexico, in April 1983, Sloan had returned to Florida for a second go-round as the Gators' head coach.

He left N.C. State in a huff with athletics director Willis Casey, with whom he had a stormy relationship that could be traced back to the day that longtime N.C. State athletics director Roy Clogston died in 1969. Both Casey, the swimming coach at State, and Sloan pursued the job. Sloan got the first offer, and accepted until he found out that he would have to give up his job as basketball coach. He backed out two days later, after consulting with his wife.

AP/WWP

NORM SLOAN 59

> "Personally, I wish he could have stayed and created a legacy like Dean Smith did at North Carolina and Mike Krzyzewski has done at Duke. But that was something between Coach Sloan and Willis Casey. I don't know why they didn't see eye to eye more."

[TOMMY BURLESON]

Casey became the athletics director, but Sloan always refused to call him "Boss."

A decade later, after three ACC titles and the school's first national championship, Sloan discovered that he and his staff were among the lowest paid coaches in the league. He had already been contacted by Florida, where Sloan had coached from 1960-66, about the vacancy left by John Lotz, when Casey and N.C. State president Joab Thomas started talking about a contract extension and a raise.

But with Casey out of town, Sloan went to Dr. Thomas, told him about the Florida offer and requested a raise for himself and his staff. When Casey found out about it, he thought Sloan was bluffing. He wasn't.

"He really wanted to stay here, but they didn't match the salaries until the last minute, after he had already accepted the job at Florida and he couldn't back down," Joan Sloan says. "We had a family, and State was not willing to up the salaries for anybody."

After building a SEC-champion program at Florida, Sloan and his staff were forced to resign just before the beginning of the 1989-90 season, amid DEA and NCAA investigations about the school's drug-testing program and allegations of giving cash to players. Sloan was bitter about the way his career ended, mainly because he thought he didn't get the support he needed from the Florida administration and athletics director. But he settled back into life in the North Carolina mountains near Newland, one pine-covered peak from where Burleson lives.

Sloan later said he regretted leaving N.C. State, and many of his players felt the same way.

"Personally, I wish he could have stayed and created a legacy like Dean Smith did at North Carolina and Mike Krzyzewski has done at Duke," Burleson says. "But that was something between Coach Sloan and Willis Casey. I don't know why they didn't see eye to eye more."

When Sloan died of pulmonary fibrosis on December 9, 2003, the Atlantic Coast Conference lost one of its most fiery and emotional characters, a guy whose character was just as colorful as those red, black and yellow plaid jackets he used to wear on the sidelines. Sloan compiled a 627-395 record during his coaching career and was named Coach of the Year in both the Southern Conference and the ACC. He built one of the ACC's greatest teams with Thompson, Towe and Burleson and won the league's second national championship.

> ## "He should be remembered as a great, great coach. Because that's what he was."
>
> [MONTE TOWE]

Yet, the mournful lament for those who gathered to say goodbye at Edenton Street United Methodist Church for his funeral was that Sloan never got the credit he deserved for being one of the top coaches in college basketball history. He's in the North Carolina Sports Hall of Fame and in the Indiana Basketball Hall of Fame. But, with two probations on his record, he may never make it into the National Basketball Hall of Fame.

"I just want people to realize what a great coach he was," Burleson says. "He was a little bit fiery, of course. You didn't always agree with him, but you never won an argument with him, either. But he was the perfect coach for our team."

At his funeral, when Stormin' Norman finally calmed down, his friends and former players enjoyed retelling the best stories about one of the ACC's most intense characters. For some, however, there is more to Sloan's legacy than just that plaid-clad persona.

"He should be remembered as a great, great coach," says Towe, now the head coach at New Orleans. "Because that's what he was."

VANN
WILLIFORD

V ann Williford was so anxious to sign a letter of intent to play basketball at N.C. State, he interrupted Wolfpack coach Norm Sloan in the middle of a round of golf at Pinehurst.

Williford, a lanky boy of six foot six with slim Division I prospects, had his mother drive him over from the family's home in Fayetteville, North Carolina, to catch up with Sloan, who was at the famed golf resort in the Sandhills for the ACC golf tournament. When Sloan finished putting out on the ninth green—Williford doesn't remember which of the resorts courses—the young boy and his widowed mother were there waiting with a pen in hand.

For years, Williford dreamed of playing in Reynolds Coliseum, home of the Dixie Classic and the basketball palace where boyhood idols like Ronnie Shavlik and Lou Pucillo played.

Playing on the courts around Fort Bragg, Williford developed into a capable, but skinny, forward that helped Fayetteville High School win back-to-back Class AAAA state championships. Williford was a complementary player on the first championship squad, because teammate Rusty Clark, who later played at North Carolina, was the undisputed star for a team that was expected to win it all in the state's highest division. But the second title was a surprise, won in the final seconds by a pair of Williford free throws.

Still, there were no recruiting skirmishes for Williford, whose spindly frame was bypassed during his senior season by all the coaches on Tobacco Road. Then-Wolfpack coach Press Maravich had

VANN WILLIFORD

Born: January 26, 1958 (Fayetteville, North Carolina)
High School: Fayetteville High School
Degree: B.S., Industrial Engineering, N.C. State, 1970.
Position: Forward
Number: 14 (honored)
Years with the Wolfpack: 1967-70
NCAA Tournament Appearances: 1970
Championships: 1965, '66 North Carolina High School 4-A Championship; 1970 ACC Championship
Honors:
★ 1966 Most Valuable Player North Carolina 4-A State Championship
★ Led ACC in field goal percentage in 1968 at 57.3 percent
★ 1969 and '70 first-team All-ACC selection
★ 1968, '70 first-team All-ACC Tournament
★ 1969 Second-team All-ACC Tournament
★ 1970 Everett Case Award winner (ACC Tournament Most Valuable Player)
★ 1970 All-ACC Tournament selection
★ 1970 All-East Region Team
★ 1970 ACC All-Academic selection
★ 1970 East-West All-Star Game
★ 1969 H.C. Kennett Award
★ 1969 Outstanding All-Around Student Athlete Award
★ 1969, '70 Jon Speaks Award winner
★ 1970 Alumni Athletic Trophy winner
★ 1970 NBA third-round draft pick (Phoenix Suns, 48th overall)

absolutely no interest in Williford because Maravich's son, Pete, was all set to become the next Wolfpack star.

But funny things happen in basketball and in life: Maravich never played a game for the Wolfpack, and Williford was the guy who led State to its first ACC Championship under Sloan.

Maravich, the basketball prodigy who grew up dribbling through the streets of

"That would have been the kiss of death had it happened."

[VANN WILLIFORD]

Clemson, South Carolina, and was a superstar at Raleigh's Broughton High School, couldn't get admitted into N.C. State. The ACC had a steadfast rule that all athletes had to score at least 800 on the SAT, and even after a year at prep school, Maravich couldn't make the score.

So father and son headed off to the academically less restrictive Southeastern Conference, to coach and play at Louisiana State. That left the Wolfpack needing a coach and more than just the one recruit, Nelson Isley, that Coach Maravich had bagged before he bagged it.

Williford, the youngest of three children who needed a scholarship if he had any hopes of going to college, learned the game by tagging along with his big brother, Richard, to various industrial league basketball games around Fayetteville.

"He was a very good high school player and used to play in all the industrial leagues," Williford says. "I would go with him to these games, and during timeouts and halftimes and between games, I would be shooting on the sidelines. He piqued my interest in the game."

Williford honed his fundamentals playing pickup games with his buddies in and around the courts at Bragg, getting a big taste of basketball and a touch of experience

with the military that would serve him at N.C. State when he enrolled in the ROTC program.

By the time high school was over, Williford had some interest from Western Carolina and Pfeiffer and a possible appointment to the U.S. Naval Academy. He ended up committing with Pfeiffer, but told coach Francis Essix plainly: "If I get a better offer, I am going elsewhere."

By late spring, it began to look like there would be no better offers, until Sloan, a State alumni who had built a successful program at Florida, began to assess the program he inherited from Maravich. Sloan asked his coaches if there were any unsigned players still available. William Bell, a big Wolfpack booster from Fayetteville, packed Williford and an eight-millimeter film of Fayetteville playing against Durham High School and six-foot-10 center Randy Denton.

Sloan watched the film while Bill Kretzer walked a giddy Williford around campus. The coach called a few days later to offer Williford a scholarship, and it didn't take long for Vann to make a decision. He easily would have driven a golf cart from Fayetteville to Pinehurst to sign the papers.

For more than a year, it appeared that those doubters who didn't think Williford could play at the highest level of college basketball were right. He struggled as a freshman, and Sloan openly discussed redshirting Williford as a sophomore.

"That would have been the kiss of death had it happened," Williford says. "He was going to go after his players. If I had been redshirted, I think I would have wound up sitting on the bench for three or four years and not played at all."

Williford went back to Fayetteville for the summer and worked every day on his game, while working in the town's summer recreation department. When he got back to campus for the 1967-68 season, Williford teamed with Kretzer as a double post in Sloan's continuity offense. He averaged only 11.2 points, but even as an undersized center, Williford hustled his way to an eight-rebound-per-game average and led the ACC in field goal percentage by making 57.3 percent of his shots.

A half-dozen games into the season, he was not only out of redshirt contention, he was in the starting lineup. It was a big surprise for everybody, including Williford, who was so nervous in his ACC debut that he put his gym shorts on backwards in the locker room.

At the end of the year, Williford and Kretzer were principle figures in one of the most bizarre and controversial ACC Tournament games ever played. Sloan started the semifinal game against sixth-ranked and regular-season runner-up Duke with his two post players at the top of the key, daring Blue Devil coach Vic Bubas to bring his big man, Mike Lewis, from under the basket. Bubas refused, and the result was a dead-air game that mostly featured Kretzer at midcourt dribbling the basketball.

Players from both teams caught up with each other in on-court conversations, a referee sat on the scorers table and Bubas refused to allow Lewis to budge from under the basket.

"This is as exciting as watching artificial insemination," UNC radio announcer Bill Currie said on the air.

Williford scored a single free throw with 16 seconds remaining, giving the Wolfpack an 11-9 lead, and each team scored a single free throw the rest of the way, finishing off the fabled "12-10 Game."

But no strategy could help the Wolfpack in the title game against North Carolina: the Tar Heels won 87-50, in what was then the largest winning margin in the title game in the tournament's history.

That game was also marred early in the second half when Williford and UNC's Clark, the two old Fayetteville High teammates, ended up in a tussle that resulted in Williford being knocked out when Clark hit him in the back of the head, earning him an ejection and cooling what had always been a cordial relationship.

"We aren't any less friends than we were and we aren't any more friends, because we weren't very close, anyway," Williford said.

As a junior, Williford developed his offensive skills and was named first-team All-ACC, thanks in part to his relationship with burly guard Rick Anheuser, who had transferred the previous year from Bradley University.

"Norm made Anheuser better than he ever was, and Anheuser and Norm helped Vann become the player he was," former Wolfpack assistant Sam Esposito says. "Vann kept getting better and better, and Anheuser had a lot to do with it. Before that, he was just sort of out there to play.

"They played a lot of two-on-two."

Williford, the virtually unwanted recruit, was a first-team All-ACC selection as a junior and one of the best players in the league as a senior, when the Wolfpack won 16 of its first 17 games and was ranked as high as fifth in the nation. But that was the season that belonged to South Carolina, which the consensus preseason No. 1 and never dropped lower than eighth in the polls. The Gamecocks, led by former North Carolina coach Frank McGuire, recorded the third unbeaten ACC regular-season mark by going 14-0 in the conference.

With the NCAA East regional slated to be in Columbia, South Carolina, the Gamecocks headed into Charlotte for the 1970 ACC Tournament with the kind of swagger that could only be taught by McGuire, the New York-born coach who was lured South in the 1950s to challenge Everett Case's supremacy in the ACC.

McGuire did it, winning the NCAA championship in 1957 with the undefeated Tar Heels, but left the school in 1960 for the NBA's New York Knicks when the gambling scandals broke. But he came back to the ACC to build South Carolina into a national power, and 1970 was the year that his loaded team was supposed to rule the roost.

But star shooting guard John Roche turned his ankle in the semifinal game

> **"Norm absolutely outcoached McGuire. They came in the game with the attitude that they could play with anybody on their terms. It was pure coaching genius."**
>
> [VANN WILLIFORD]

against Wake Forest, and the Wolfpack turned McGuire's dreams of his second national title into a nightmare, thanks again to Sloan's slow-down tactics that negated the Gamecocks' massive size advantage.

Still, South Carolina led by as many as 11 points in the first half and was ahead 24-17 at halftime. Despite the deficit, Sloan ordered his team to hold the ball early in the second half, and nearly six minutes ticked off the clock before McGuire finally pulled his team out of its 2-1-2 zone. It turned out to be a huge mistake.

Williford keyed a comeback that allowed the Wolfpack to tie the game at 35 in regulation. Two overtimes later, after Wolfpack guard Ed Leftwich stole the ball at midcourt from Gamecock point guard Bobby Cremins, State had won its first ACC

for some solace. Because of NCAA rules at the time, since the Gamecocks were hosting an NCAA Regional, they could not play in the National Invitation Tournament.

"That was one of the toughest moments of my life," Cremins said when he was the head coach at Georgia Tech. "We had such a great team. It made life miserable for us and Coach McGuire. I was just miserable."

But on the other side of the court, the emotions were exactly opposite. Sloan, an original Case recruit who loved the tradition established by his old mentor, became the third N.C. State coach to win an ACC championship. And Williford won the award named after the former coach.

Even now, Williford gets choked up about Sloan's gamble to give him a scholarship, based solely on an eight-millimeter film. That point was driven home in 1999 when athletics director Les Robinson went to Sloan and asked which of his players deserved to have his jersey honored by the school.

Williford, Sloan's first recruit and an unexpected star of the league, was the first name the coach mentioned.

"I think he appreciated what I did for him as much as I appreciated what he did for me," Williford says.

title under Sloan. Williford was named the tournament's Most Valuable Player, after scoring 18 points in the title game.

"Norm absolutely outcoached McGuire," Williford said. "They came in the game with the attitude that they could play with anybody on their terms. It was pure coaching genius."

McGuire refused to let his team come out of the locker room to accept the second-place trophy, and Cremins disappeared after the game into the North Carolina mountains

"I think he appreciated what I did for him as much as I appreciated what he did for me."

[VANN WILLIFORD]

The Wolfpack's appearance in the 1970 NCAA Tournament was a let down. Playing on South Carolina's home court, with the entire arena against it, the Wolfpack lost to St. Bonaventure in the opening game, and then to Niagara in the consolation contest.

Williford, who signed up to join the army when he enrolled in advanced ROTC at State, was drafted in the fourth round of the ABA draft by the Carolina Cougars. He played two years for the troubled franchise, but it did not turn out to be the same kind of success story as his college career.

"Other than the money I made, my professional career was not a very pleasant experience," Williford says.

In the end, following a two-year stint as a second lieutenant in his home town at Fort Bragg, Williford used his N.C. State contacts, and the money he made from his Cougars contract, to build a lifelong career in industrial equipment sales. For more than three decades, he has been president of Atlantic Coast Toyotalift in High Point, North Carolina.

"It's been a good life," Williford says.

TOMMY
BURLESON

The machine gun in the German guard's hand made the long trip from the small of Tommy Burleson's back to the base of his skull very quickly.

"Face the wall and do not turn around," the guard said in perfect English.

All the seven-foot-two basketball center could do was look way down at this feet and pray. Oddly, what he sees now when he closes his eyes and thinks about this moment more than three decades ago is the imperfections in the concrete wall. He wonders: Would he approve such a wall nowadays?

Fear etches the weirdest memories on the brain.

"I was scared for my life," Burleson says. "I just prayed."

What haunts him, though, is that he only prayed for himself. Who wouldn't? Here he was, an 18-year-old kid from Newland, North Carolina, (population: 564) trying to get to his dorm room at the 1972 Olympics in Munich, Germany. Behind him—and behind the guard with the automatic rifle in his hand—were nine sobbing Israeli athletes and coaches who were being led to a helicopter by eight Palestinian terrorists.

Not long after Burleson, three German guards and two Italian athletes watched the helicopter fly away, there was a botched rescue attempt at the NATO air base in Firstenfeldbruck and all nine Israelis—along with two of their captors—died.

"I can still close my eyes right now and see that green helicopter and those red lights flashing as it left the compound," Burleson says.

More than 30 years of introspection later, remembering that flashing bird disap-

TOMMY BURLESON

Born: February 24, 1952 (Crossnore, North Carolina)
High School: Avery County High School, Newland, North Carolina
Degree: B.S., Agricultural Economics, N.C. State, 1974
Position: Center
Number: 24 (honored)
Years with the Wolfpack: 1970-74
NCAA Tournament Appearances: 1974
Championships: 1973, '74 ACC Tournament Championship; 1974 NCAA Championship
Honors:
★ Second in school history with 1,066 career rebounds
★ Led ACC in rebounding in 1972 at 14.0 rebounds per game, '73 at 12.0 rebounds per game
★ 1972 Olympic team (silver medal)
★ 1972, '73 First-team All-ACC selection
★ 1973, '73 First-team All-ACC Tournament
★ 1973 Everett Case Award winner (ACC Tournament Most Valuable Player)
★ 1974 Second-team All-ACC selection
★ 1974 Everett Case Award winner (ACC Tournament Most Valuable Player)
★ 1974 Jon Speaks Award winner
★ 1974 NBA first-round draft pick (Seattle SuperSonics, third overall)
★ 1974 Alumni Athletic Trophy winner
★ Member of the ACC 50th Anniversary team

pear in the distance and realizing what happened to its occupants helps Burleson put into proper perspective the unbelievable highs and disappointing lows that defined his sometimes crazy career in athletics.

"It was just our misfortune that we lost a basketball game," says Burleson, referring to the subsequent defeat of the United States to the Soviet Union, in one of the most controversial outcomes of the modern Olympics. "The true tragedy was that 11

"I got over the game pretty quickly. I was more upset that I wasn't allowed to play in the gold medal game."

[TOMMY BURLESON]

Israel coaches and athletes went back to their homes in caskets and boxes."

Burleson didn't contribute much to that '72 U.S. Olympic team, which has left its silver medal locked away in a vault in Switzerland since that controversial game in 1972. He was the second-lowest scoring player on the team. He was benched in the gold medal game for being caught with his fiancée on the balcony of his dorm room at the Olympic village, a violation of U.S. coach Henry Iba's team rules.

In the final moments of that game, following Doug Collins's groggy free throws that gave the U.S. a 50-49 lead, all hell began to break loose, thanks to an unprompted horn and confusion at the scorer's table. Burleson begged Iba to go into the game to guard the Soviet basket.

"No, you're benched," Iba told him.

In the days before the terrorist incident, assistant coach John Bach had discovered that Burleson was giving his fiancée a tour of his dorm room, and found them on the balcony looking over the Olympic Village.

"Other players have had their mothers and sisters in here," Burleson said, as his defense. "And the dorm is not restricted to just males. I just showed her our room."

"Fine," Bach said. "I won't tell Coach Iba about it."

Burleson forgot about it, but apparently Iba found out, and he wouldn't budge from his decision to bench Burleson. The young center pleaded with both Bach and assistant coach Don Haskins of Texas-El Paso to convince the head coach to insert him into the lineup to defend the Soviet basket in those final three seconds.

"You have got to get me into the game to guard (Aleksander) Belov," Burleson said. "The other guys are too small to guard Belov. You have got to put me in the game."

"No," Bach told him, "you've been benched."

Watch the tape of the final seconds of that game, and as game officials and FIBA General Secretary R. William Jones twice make the decision to put three seconds back on the clock, giving the Russians their double mulligan at ending the USA's 67-game winning streak in the Olympics, you can see a seething Burleson standing with his arms crossed. He's not mad about the decision to put time on the clock.

"I got over the game pretty quickly," Burleson said. "I was more upset that I wasn't allowed to play in the gold medal game."

To this day, Burleson is convinced he could have helped defend Belov, and preserved the Americans' Olympic winning streak. And if there is anything that "The Newland Needle" leaves as his basketball legacy it is this: once he convinced himself of something, there was no changing his mind.

Ask Len Elmore, the Maryland center who told reporters after outplaying Burleson in a regular-season game that they should go tell Burleson "that I am THE center in the ACC." Wolfpack coach Norm Sloan clipped that nugget out of the paper. The day of the 1974 ACC Tournament championship game, after the media had named Elmore to the league's first-team and Burleson to the second-team all-conference squad, Sloan pulled the clipping out of his wallet and had assistant Eddie Biedenbach tape it to Burleson's locker, before the Wolfpack played Maryland. An inspired, and thoroughly motivated, Burleson went out and had the greatest individual performance in the greatest game ever played in ACC history, making 18 of his 25 field goal attempts and winning his second consecutive Everett Case Award as the tournament Most Valuable Player.

Ask Luke Witte, the former Ohio State center who lost a head-to-head battle with Burleson for the final spot on the '72 Olympic roster. The two were among 75 college players who were pared down during the trials in Colorado Springs, competing for the center position that probably should have gone to Bill Walton. But Walton refused to try out for the team, opening the door for Burleson to become the first N.C. State player to ever make an Olympic basketball roster. The competition between Witte and Burleson came

down to the final scrimmage, with the winner going to the final training camp in Pearl Harbor, Hawaii.

"(Kentucky's) Joe B. Hall was coaching Luke's team and (Wright Junior College's) Ed Badger was coaching our team," Burleson remembers. "A good friend of mine, Kermit Washington, was on their team. Joe B. Hall had told them that Kermit should double-down on me every time I got the ball.

"Kermit and I had worked Red Auerbach's camps and stuff and we were good friends, and still are. He came to me and said, 'I am going to double down on you, but don't worry, go ahead and take your hook shot because I am not going to try to slap at the ball or block your shot or anything like that. Go ahead and take your shot.'

"It wasn't a conspiracy or anything, it's just that Kermit felt it was unfair his team was going to double-team me, and we were not going to double-team Witte. It became more of a one-on-one battle."

Burleson had 18 points and 13 rebounds to Witte's three points and 11 rebounds, and Burleson became the youngest player to make the Olympic roster.

"Burleson is one of the great competitors that I ever coached," Sloan said during a 1999 interview. "So much so that he couldn't get himself up for what he didn't consider a challenge. 'What do I have to prove?' The only thing I told Tommy was that when the end of the season came around that he could keep himself off the all-conference team. Sure enough he did.

N.C. State Student Media Authority/*Technician*

"Tommy doesn't even realize how much of a transformation he went through, beginning with those Olympic Games. I am not even going to attempt to explain Tommy Burleson to you. He is a very complex person. He had an inferiority complex coming out of high school. Typical of people like that, he was very competitive. The problem with Tommy was getting him started. Tommy was reluctant to go out there and prove what he could do for fear he wouldn't do it. This was the only problem with Tommy Burleson. Once he got over that, he was a son of a gun."

That's perhaps the mildest—especially for Sloan—way to put it.

But it was difficult for some to ever think of Burleson as anything other than a freak of genes, a skinny stick of a farm boy born to a six-foot-two father and a five-foot-10 mother. The baby who weighed 10 pounds, three ounces, and was 23 inches long at birth became a giant who brought his mountainous demeanor to the flatlands and was the first, and most important, piece for a team that is remembered as one of the best in the history of college basketball.

Burleson, while on a trip to Raleigh with his 4-H club, landed on Coach Sloan's doorstep as a near gift. Burleson was walking around campus with his uncle, Ben Ware, one afternoon during the N.C. State Agriculture and Life Science Department's Open House. They had gone to see Glassy the Cow, the famous bovine with a window implanted on her side to show the innerworkings of her four stomachs, earlier in the day in the open field adjacent to Reynolds Coliseum.

Burleson loved walking around the campus with Ben, and his other uncle, June,

who both went to school at State. Burleson remembers going to the first game ever played at Carter-Finley Stadium in 1966. As a kid, growing up on his family's 14-acre farm, Burleson always knew he wanted to study Agriculture at State College.

So this summer afternoon, Burleson and Ware stopped by the basketball office. They talked to Charlie Bryant, one of Sloan's assistants, who was immediately excited about a 14-year-old eighth-grader who already stood six-foot-eight.

"Yeah, send him in," Sloan said.

When Burleson bent down to enter the door, he had the head coach's attention.

"We had heard about him but we didn't know too much about him," said Sam Esposito, who doubled as N.C. State's baseball coach and an assistant on Sloan's basketball staff. "We had just started at the school. Burleson walked in and he had to bend down to keep from hitting his head coming in the door. We almost had a heart attack."

Duke and North Carolina pursued Burleson from the beginning as well, but in the back of his mind Burleson didn't think he could play for those schools, who were becoming regulars in the Top 10 and at the Final Four with coaches Vic Bubas and Dean Smith. Besides, many hours of walking among the bricks on the Raleigh campus bonded Burleson's heart to State, and the 367 other schools that sent letters of interest about Burleson's services couldn't compete with that.

Burleson told Sloan early on that he would attend State, but he did not want to make the announcement public. At the time,

> # "I just wanted to be a part of N.C. State basketball. I didn't think I was good enough to play at Carolina. I didn't think I was good enough to play at Duke. I just wanted to be a good ball player."

[TOMMY BURLESON]

the young center was working at Grandfather Mountain for Hugh Morton, the owner of the mountain and a passionate photographer and Carolina basketball fan.

When Burleson signed with the Wolfpack following his senior basketball season, Dean Smith was furious, accusing Sloan of hiding the commitment.

"They didn't tell anybody," Smith says. "Maybe Norm wanted me to spend my time recruiting (Tommy) instead of anybody else. I spent a lot of time going to the mountains to show interest."

According to Burleson, his commitment assured that the Wolfpack would also get David Thompson. The two became friendly while playing against each other in high school in the Western North Carolina High School Athletics Association. Burleson said they made a pact to go to college together, something Sloan never accepted as gospel.

"I asked David one time why he came to N.C. State," Burleson says. "He said 'Because you did.'"

"I just wanted to be a part of N.C. State basketball. I didn't think I was good enough to play at Carolina. I didn't think I was good

enough to play at Duke. I just wanted to be a good ball player."

And that's what so many other people wanted for him too. They figured, here's a guy who is seven feet, four inches tall. Why doesn't he dominate every game? As a sophomore, the knobby-kneed Burleson lost the ACC scoring title to Virginia's Barry Parkhill by three-tenths of a point and he led the league in rebounding at 14.0 per game.

"After that, people were starting to wonder if he was ever going to cut loose," Sloan said.

But Burleson has always been a complicated fellow, one who was prone to feel sorry for himself in earlier days. That's what he was feeling in May 1972, about three months after he accidentally found a key to three pinball machines in the lobby of Sullivan dormitory. Burleson, with two older sisters living at home, came from a poor background. He never had an allowance in his four years at State, and there was little opportunity for spending money after the NCAA did away with the $15 per month in laundry money that athletes used to receive as part of their scholarships.

So, in a rage of self-pity, Burleson and Bruce A. Schneider broke into the machines and took $117 in change. Feeling guilty, he was in Sloan's office the next day to confess to his coach, who told Burleson to go turn himself in. To this day, Burleson considers it one of the lowest points of his life, especially after going to court and seeing the two children of the man who owned the machines.

"I realized I was taking food out of their mouths," he says. "I was messing with his livelihood. I've never felt lower in my life."

He even wrote a letter to all the members of the Wolfpack Club apologizing for his transgression.

While most people consider David Thompson the greatest player in ACC basketball history, Burleson was the most important centerpiece in building a program, an unstoppable inside player with a sweeping hook shot. After he came, Thompson followed, and then Sloan found Towe.

Burleson had many detractors during his career, and he always enjoyed showing to people that he was actually quite athletic, despite his gangly frame. As a center fielder at Avery County High School, Burleson says he hit .556 on the baseball team. He shot in the 80s on the golf course before he outgrew his clubs and he could bowl over 200 regularly. He took up juggling to improve his coordination and, from the time he began to grow four inches per year between the ages 13-17, he lifted weights hid dad bought him out of the Sears catalogue. Had his father not forbidden it, Burleson would have played football, too.

"There are still people who don't think Tommy was a great athlete," Sloan said. "Opponents naturally belittled him. He read stuff that said he was gawdy and uncoordinated, and he believed him. But we never once had to wait on him."

Despite the snub by the media in his senior season, Burleson is one of only three players in ACC history two win back-to-back ACC Tournament Most Valuable Player Awards and is now remembered as one of the greatest competitors the league has ever known.

Burleson's professional career ended up as a bust. He was the third overall pick of the 1974 draft, taken by the Seattle SuperSonics, but he never matched the same kind of competitive fire he had in college. On Valentine's Day 1979, Burleson tore three of the four ligaments in his left knee, and had to undergo experimental surgery to reconstruct the damage.

"I messed up my pro career, and I blame myself," Burleson says. "I go out in my first exhibition game and scored 44 points. Spencer Haywood and Fred Brown walked over to me and said, 'You are not going to score 44 points again. We are not going to throw you the ball.'

"I didn't go into with the same thinking I used at N.C. State. Here I was, the No. 3 draft choice and I was playing with a great team. I had good numbers, but I really didn't use my talents the way I should have. I didn't pass the ball the way I could have, and I let some things off the court get me off track. It was a lack of wisdom."

Burleson doesn't like to discuss his off-court problems, but his first marriage ended and he admits that, like his good friend David Thompson, he engaged in some self-destructive behavior.

> # "I let some personal problems take away from my focus. To play at that level, the game has to be your total life. You can't be worrying about what is taking place at your house, or what you are doing with your friends. You need to be totally focused."
>
> [TOMMY BURLESON]

"I just wasn't really into the game the way I should have been," Burleson says.

"I let some personal problems take away from my focus. To play at that level, the game has to be your total life. You can't be worrying about what is taking place at your house, or what you are doing with your friends. You need to be totally focused."

The *Rocky Mountain News* once listed Burleson, along with infamous N.C. State product Chris Washburn, among the 10 worst No. 3 draft picks in NBA history. That's a little harsh, considering Washburn's problems were self-induced, and Burleson's were more injury related.

Burleson, after retiring in 1981 and becoming a devout Christian the following year, went back to his hometown of Newland, bought into a successful electrical supply business, raced speedboats as a hobby and is now the director of the Avery County Inspections and Planning Department.

Why did the seven-foot giant race speedboats? Mainly because he lost strength in his left leg after his knee surgery and couldn't properly work the clutch on the dirt-track cars he once raced. He switched to the water, where he raced power boats at upwards of 150 miles per hour. He had several spectacular crashes, including "the best wreck of the 1985 Nationals in Illinois." He finished third in the nationals in 1993, then dry docked his boat for good.

"That became my competitive outlet," Burleson says. "My basketball career came to a pretty abrupt end, and I was still craving the adrenaline rush that came from racing."

Now, Burleson has settled back among the mountains he loved so much growing up, raising his three sons and a few acres of Christmas trees. He's a fixture on the sidelines at Wolfpack basketball games, standing out like a periscope on the fourth row of the RBC Center.

DAVID
THOMPSON

Ida Thompson always worried about her baby flying too high. She, like everybody else in the world of college basketball in the early 1970s, marveled at how the youngest of her 11 children could just take off and soar, higher than anyone had ever seen. But, while others were awed by her son's unique talents, she was never able to hide her mother's concern.

"That boy is going to hurt himself," she said many times to Norm Sloan.

But, as David Thompson found out in his game-changing, above-the-rim career, it wasn't the flying that was the problem. It was coming down.

So on that March afternoon in 1974, as Thompson lay on the floor of Reynolds Coliseum in twin puddles of blood and urine—a sure sign of a devastating head injury—the world thought the greatest basketball player in ACC history was dead, having outjumped his many talents. CBS News' Walter Cronkite was on the phone with emergency room personnel at Rex Hospital as they checked out the Wolfpack's fallen star, ready to give somber reports to the nation about the player who leaped to fame a year earlier simply because he was so much better than everybody else.

The thing about this tumble, and the much more sinister one that came years later, was that it was so unlike David, the soft-spoken, polite-as-a-preacher young man who never got angry. But on this afternoon, competition took over. The Wolfpack had to get to the 1974 Final Four. It had been denied the opportunity the year before, because of an NCAA probation relating to Thompson's recruitment that kept the only undefeated

DAVID THOMPSON

Born: July 13, 1953 (Boiling Springs, North Carolina)
High School: Crest High School, Shelby, North Carolina.
Degree: B.S. Sociology, N.C. State, 2003
Position: Guard
Number: 44 (retired)
Years with the Wolfpack: 1972-75
NCAA Tournament Appearances: 1974
Championships: 1973, '74 ACC Championships; 1974 NCAA Championship
Honors:
★ Established school record with a 29.9-point scoring average in 1975
★ Owns school record for highest career scoring average at 26.8 points per game
★ Led ACC in scoring in 1973 at 24.7 points per game, '74 at 26.0 points per game, '75 at 29.0 points per game
★ 1971 North Carolina High School Player of the Year
★ Most Valuable Player, 1971 East-West All-Star Game
★ 1973 World University Games Most Valuable Player
★ 1973, '74, '75 ACC Player of the Year
★ 1973, '74, '75 First-team All-ACC selection
★ 1973, '74, '75 First-team All-ACC Tournament
★ 1973, '75 ACC Athlete of the Year
★ 1973, '74 H.C. Kennett Award winner
★ 1974 AP National Player of the Year
★ 1974 AP, UPI, USBWA, NABC, Sporting News National Player of the Year
★ 1974 Final Four Most Valuable Player
★ 1974 All-Final Four team
★ ACC Player of the Year (1973, '74, '75)
★ 1975 Alumni Athletic Trophy winner
★ 1975 Winner of the Rupp Award, Naismith Award, Eastman Kodak Award
★ 1975 NBA draft pick (Atlanta Hawks, first overall pick)
★ 1975 ABA draft pick (Virginia Squires, ninth overall pick)
★ 1976 ABA Rookie of the Year
★ 1976 ABA All-Star Game Most Valuable Player
★ 1977, '78 First-team All-NBA
★ Four-time NBA All-Star
★ 1979 NBA All-Star Game Most Valuable Player Jerseys retired: No. 44 at Crest High School, No. 44 at N.C. State, No. 33 at Denver Nuggets

"That was a reckless act on my part. That just shows that you shouldn't lose control on the basketball court.

[DAVID THOMPSON]

team in school history from going to the NCAA Tournament. It had to get a rematch with UCLA, the most dominant program in college basketball history that had embarrassed Thompson and the Wolfpack earlier in the season in a made-for-television special in St. Louis. But to make that short ride from Raleigh to Greensboro, the site of the Final Four, the Pack had to get past Pittsburgh.

So, if the officials were going to let Pitt slap Thompson on the arm on every shot, then he was going to make sure no Panther player got off an uncontested shot, even if he had to get uncharacteristically mad.

Midway through the first half of this NCAA East Region final at Reynolds Coliseum, someone slapped Thompson's arm yet again, and his shot came up about two feet short. He was enraged. He ran down the court with only one goal: to block Pitt's next shot. And he did, tipping the ball well after it left Keith Starr's hands. As an official called goaltending, Thomson's foot caught the corner of six-foot-eight teammate Phil Spence's shoulder. It may have been as high as Thompson, whose 44-inch vertical leap had been certified by the *Guinness Book of World Records*, ever flew on the basketball court.

He flipped in mid-air, landing with his neck perpendicular to his body. When teammate Tommy Burleson saw the replay of what happened to his friend, he got physically ill.

"That was a reckless act on my part," Thompson says. "That just shows that you

shouldn't lose control on the basketball court. I had always been cool under pressure. I got a little upset, which was out of character for me, and I paid a huge price for it."

He was carried off the floor on a stretcher, the crowd silenced and terrified. He regained consciousness just behind Case Athletic Center, and the first person he recognized was his mom.

"My mother always said one day I was going to hurt myself," Thompson says. "And I guess I did."

As it turned out of course, that fall to the wooden floor didn't come close to killing Thompson, whose muscular physique probably spared him a massive head trauma. He was well enough a week—and 15 stitches to his head—later to block Bill Walton's shot twice in the Wolfpack's double-overtime victory over UCLA in the NCAA Tournament semifinals and to score 21 points in the championship game against Marquette.

But a different kind of fall did ruin Thompson's career and reputation. It just wasn't on the court. Basketball and his tal-

"God brought me to my knees so I could look up to him. When I was at the top of my career, the more successful I became, the further I got away from the Lord."

[DAVID THOMPSON]

ents in the game brought him the fame, the money and the notoriety that steered Thompson into the worst of all the athletic clichés: drug addiction.

And the drugs dropped Thompson flatter than the fall that afternoon against Pittsburgh. Now, nearly 20 years after Thompson survived the humiliation of jail and financial ruin, he believes that was God's plan all along.

"God brought me to my knees so I could look up to Him," Thomson says in his often repeated inspirational speech that he gives to youth clinics and civic groups. "When I was at the top of my career, the more successful I became, the further I got away from the Lord."

Because of the drugs and injuries, Thompson's career came to an abrupt and embarrassing ending. Sometimes, when he stands in front of a new generation of basketball fans who have no idea about his groundbreaking abilities, he puts his career into the only context they might understand: he was Michael Jordan's hero.

Drugs cost Thompson nearly everything: his unmatchable talent, his personal fortune, his family and his friends. Even after he was given another chance to land safely on his feet, thanks to his position as the director

of community relations with the Charlotte Hornets, he nearly gave it all back again, needing another round of rehabilitation in the late 1980s to fight an alcohol problem that came with returning to the spotlight in his home state.

Thompson, professional basketball's first million-dollar player, remembers the first time he did cocaine. It was during the 1976 ABA Championship series against the New York Nets, as Thompson tried to match Julius "Dr. J" Erving dunk for high-flying dunk. He had already played more than 100 games that season, and he carried the fatigue like ankle weights.

"I tried it and I liked it," Thompson says of the cocaine. "I was a little apprehensive at first. The next year, at a lot of the parties and a lot of the functions I went to it was readily available. Once you break down and give in, it's a lot easier to do it the next time. Before you know it, it becomes a habit.

"It started on a social level and it became an addiction."

This was not the same David Thompson who played at N.C. State. The talent was still there and all the remarkable skills were the same. He could still jump from under the basket and grab a quarter off the top of the backboard and leave change if he needed to. But the high-flying world of professional basketball changed him.

"The thing that happened with David, I think, is that he didn't know how to say no to people," Norm Sloan said in a 1999 interview. "That was fine when he was with his friends. They knew how to take care of him. But when he got to the pros, he didn't know how to say no."

And those new friends cost Thompson his old friends, at least for a while.

For eight years, Thompson and Tommy Burleson did not speak to each other. It's something that's unfathomable to both of them now, because they have become even closer after their basketball careers ended than they were in college. In the late 1980s, while Thompson was serving 180 days in jail for assaulting his wife while freebasing cocaine, his Wolfpack teammate and one-time roommate Monte Towe had completely lost touch with the player who was the catalyst for the chemistry of the '74 championship team.

Burleson blames himself for much of Thompson's troubles. Without realizing it, he was harshly judging his old friend.

"I turned my back on David," says Burleson, who developed drinking issues and personal problems of his own during the early days of his professional career with the Seattle SuperSonics. "He and I didn't speak for about eight years there when he got involved in drugs. I was technically not into drugs, but alcohol is just as bad.

"I feel bad about that. I just stopped calling him. I can't believe I didn't try to help

him. We finally got back together, and our friendship is as strong as it ever will be."

Thompson has never felt let down by Burleson, or any of his other Wolfpack friends. He simply blames his own weaknesses for the things that happened to him during what started out as a spectacular professional career. He was the one who fell down the stairs at Studio 54 in a drug-induced haze, suffering the knee injury that ruined his career. He was the one whose comeback in 1985 ended when he was arrested for public intoxication at an Indianapolis strip bar. He was the one who sought bankruptcy protection from 41 creditors who claimed he owed them a total of $2.2 million.

"Tommy never let me down," Thompson says. "I was in my own little world. You know with a true friend, he will always be there to talk to. The love has always been there. Sometimes, the communication has not been. Mainly, that was on me for not being accessible. Communication is two ways."

Both Thompson and Burleson are now deeply religious, and share their message about the highs and lows of their basketball career to young people.

"We turned our lives over to Christ," Thompson says. "We try to make a difference in young people's lives through basketball."

Thompson has clawed his way out of financial troubles, through motivational speaking, basketball clinics and his book, Skywalker, published in 2003.

"I am not wealthy by any means, but all my needs are being met," Thompson says.

"David was the queen on the chessboard. He could go everywhere, inside, outside, rebounding. His impact was felt all over the floor. He changed the game."

[LEN ELMORE]

"I don't really need anything. I have been able to make a decent living. I may not ever get back to where I was making a million dollars a year, but how many people do?

"Right now, my life is far better than it was then. Along with money comes problems. I am happy and I am free. I am not addicted to drugs any more. I have a lot of joy in my life. Seeing where I came from and where I am today, I am very happy and very proud. A lot of people who went through what I went through didn't make it."

Perhaps it was the shared experiences, the pressure to live up to the greatness of their two-year run at N.C. State, in which the Wolfpack lost only one game, that took them down a treacherous road to addiction and other problems. Perhaps it was just being part of the NBA culture during an era that nearly killed the league. Whatever the reasons, both Thompson and Burleson believe it all happened for a purpose.

"When I watch the UCLA game, especially on that one tip-in, I am sure God had a hand in us winning," Burleson says. "He was rewarding our parents and our grandparents and Mr. (Everett) Case and the generations of N.C. State people who built the foundation of the program. But I think he had another plan for us.

"I turned my back on Christ for a while, and David turned his back on Christ. God brought us back with humility. It was just part of the deal.

"We were at a meeting not long ago and David told me, 'Burl, if we hadn't traveled the paths that we did, our testimony would not be as strong today. If we had not made the mistakes that we made, then no one would listen to our message.'

"Those are some of the best words that David has ever said to me."

For those who watched him and played against him, Thompson is still remembered as the ACC's greatest player, even if the league did honor Michael Jordan as the ACC's Greatest Athlete during its 50th anniversary celebration in 2003. That offended Burleson, who believed his friend should win the honor without much debate. Many others agree.

"I still think David Thompson is the greatest player ever in college basketball," says former Maryland All-American Len Elmore, who watched as Thompson, Burleson and the rest of the Wolfpack cut down the nets at the Greensboro Coliesum following the 1974 title game that still ranks among the best college contests. "David was the queen on the chessboard. He could go everywhere, inside, outside, rebounding. His impact was felt all over the floor. He changed the game.

"Everyone from then on wanted to be a Skywalker."

Remembering his glory days at N.C. State, Thompson has only two regrets about his college career: that he only dunked the ball once and that the Wolfpack won only one national championship.

Thompson believed when he met Burleson in high school that the two could combine to create a national power in Raleigh. But State was slapped with a one-year probation in the aftermath of recruiting Thompson, primarily for minor infractions committed after Thompson signed. The NCAA found no substantive abuses that allowed the Wolfpack an advantage in recruiting Thompson, though there were numerous allegations of cash and special benefits, from a new house for Thompson's parents to the paving of the pot-hole-filled dirt road that led to the Thompson's cinder-block home in a pasture in Cleveland County.

Duke also landed on probation for one season because a Blue Devil booster, an executive at a Shelby textile mill, gave Thompson a sports jacket as a graduation gift.

Here, boiled down, are the primary violations that landed the school on probation: the school did not charge Thompson $8 a week for providing him housing while he participated in a basketball camp. He had slept

"It was tough not to be able to dunk the ball when you are way over the rim."

[DAVID THOMPSON]

on the floor of a dormitory with two friends from Shelby, Jerry and Larry Hunt. And, after Thompson signed with the Wolfpack, he played pickup games at Carmichael Gym with his future teammates. A few times, assistant basketball coach Eddie Biedenbach joined the games. The NCAA ruled those pick-up games as an illegal try-out, which Thompson considered an absurdity, considering he was one of the top recruits in the nation at the time.

"I think it was all a bunch of nitpicky stuff," Thompson said, "and I think it kept us from winning two national championships, to be honest with you.

"I think we had the team to win the championship in 1973, too."

The NCAA also prevented Wolfpack fans from seeing Thompson dunk for three years. (Or four years, for that matter, since Thompson's class was the last one that was not eligible to play as freshman, in part because of the success and interest of the N.C. State freshman team in 1972 that featured Thompson, Towe and forward Tim Stoddard.)

"It was tough not to be able to dunk the ball when you are way over the rim,"

> ## "I got a technical foul and a standing ovation at the same time. Coach Sloan took me out of the game right after that, and it was a great way to end my career at N.C. State."
>
> [DAVID THOMPSON]

Thompson said. "It would have been way easier to catch it and dunk it in one motion. I think in a lot of ways an alley oop without a dunk was a little more artistic play. You have to have body control and be able to hang in the air a little bit and make sure you didn't get it in the cylinder. It was a good play, but I would have much rather been able to throw a couple of them down and shatter a few backboards."

But in his final home game during his senior year, against UNC-Charlotte, Thompson found himself in a break-away situation late in the contest. He swooped in for a tomahawk slam, one that he made famous when winning the first ABA All-Star Game Dunk contest. And he gladly took his punishment of a technical foul, after giving the frothing fans a taste of what they had missed during his career.

"I got a technical foul and a standing ovation at the same time," Thompson says. "Coach Sloan took me out of the game right after that, and it was a great way to end my career at N.C. State."

From the time he signed his letter of intent on the hood of Biedenbach's car on a spring day in Shelby, there was never any question that Thompson would become a Wolfpack legend. But three decades after his last game, there was some concern that Thompson might never become an N.C. State graduate. He left the school in the spring of 1975 two electives short of getting his degree in sociology.

But as he watched his two daughters, Brooke and Erika, plug away at their college degrees, the old competitive fire that made Thompson so unbeatable in college began to burn again. He had to get his degree before they did. So he enrolled in the first session of summer school in 2003, then walked across the stage that December, at the same time Erika accepted her degree. A few days later, Brooke graduated from UNC-Asheville.

"It was something that bothered me for a lot of years," Thompson says of his lack of a degree. "My plan was to stay my senior year, possibly win another national championship, and get my degree. The main focus for coming back my senior year was to get my degree and graduate with my class. But when you get to the NBA, a lot of things come up..."

> **"People who come to the house, they tend to look at all the basketball stuff. But the diploma is something I am more proud of. I don't know how to explain it. It's just a feeling of completion, that's all. It completes me."**
>
> [DAVID THOMPSON]

Thompson says he was surprised at just how many people were inspired that he went back and got his degree. They still send him letters. They come up to him after one of his motivational speeches. Some of them are as old as he is. Some of them are much younger. Some of them, like Marcus Melvin, played basketball at N.C. State too.

"I guess I just didn't expect it to be that big of a deal," Thompson says.

But it hangs on the wall in the living room of Thompson's house in Charlotte, just a little higher than Brooke's and Erika's diploma. On another wall are all the awards and honors from a life devoted to basketball.

"People who come to the house, they tend to look at all the basketball stuff," Thompson said. "But the diploma is something I am more proud of. I don't know how to explain it. It's just a feeling of completion, that's all. It completes me."

Ah, finally, a safe landing.

MONTE
TOWE

onte Towe had been in this position before. He saw six other scholarship players on the N.C. State freshman team, and he knew exactly where he stood. Besides, of course, six inches shorter than everyone else.

"It was pretty clear that I was No. 7 of seven," Towe says. "I am not even sure I was very close to No. 6.

"That's the way it always was with me, being a little guy."

Several little guys have helped build the tradition of N.C. State basketball. There was Lou Pucillo, who at five-foot-nine was the shortest player ever signed to a scholarship by Everett Case. He never had any trouble scoring, and eventually became a two-time first-team all-conference player and the 1959 ACC Player of the Year.

There was also high-flying Anthony "Spud" Webb, the five foot seven satellite who could practically leap into orbit. He made his biggest splash after his college career by winning the 1986 NBA dunk contest and becoming a fan favorite for his remarkable leaping abilities.

But no diminutive guard was ever as popular as Towe, whose Davy Jones haircut and fiery personality made him the heart and soul of the Wolfpack's 1974 national championship team.

"Always being an underdog, Monte was the kind of guy who would fight you to the end, and you almost never beat him," Thompson says. "He brought that attitude, that fight, that never-say-die attitude. Monte was really that vocal leader on the court, even though Tommy (Burleson) will want to say he was the leader.

"Monte was just an extension of Coach Sloan. He exuded confidence. When it was late in the game that was something that he brought to the whole team. We always knew that Monte, Tommy or myself would some up with a big play to help us win the basketball game."

But in those first practices with his new teammates—with the recruiting class of Thompson, Tim Stoddard, Craig Kuzsmaul, Mark Moeller, John McNeely and Mike Dempsey—Towe wasn't sure he would ever get the chance he needed to prove himself.

He knew well enough that he wasn't Norm Sloan's first choice to be the point guard on a team that eventually became one

"No way am I going to take someone that size. He'll get eaten alive in the ACC."

[NORM SLOAN]

of the best in ACC and college basketball history. Sloan really wanted Baron Hill of Seymour, Indiana, who turned down the Wolfpack and went to play for Furman University.

There was even another guy whom Sloan wanted more than Towe, a fiery but small guard at Oak Hill High School in Converse, Indiana. So Sloan sent his old college roommate, Dick Dickey, a former Wolfpack All-American who lives 11 miles from Converse in Marion, Indiana, to scout a point guard named Steve Ahlfeld.

Dickey wasn't particularly impressed with Ahlfeld, but he liked Towe, who was a standout basketball, baseball and football player at Oak Hill. As an undersized quarterback, Towe led Oak Hill to back-to-back 9-0 records on the football field.

When Dickey reported back to Sloan that the coach ought to sign a five-foot-seven point guard, Sloan—as was his habit—told Dickey exactly what he thought about the idea.

"No way am I going to take someone that size," Sloan said. "He'll get eaten alive in the ACC."

Then Dickey reminded him of the story of John Mengelt. He was a six-foot-three center from Elwood, Indiana, that Dickey once suggested to Sloan. The coach declined, saying he would never have such an undersized center on his team.

Some four years later, at the end of Mengelt's All-SEC career at Auburn, he poured in 40 points against the Wolfpack in a 98-51 whipping at Auburn. Sloan told Dickey from that point on, he would take the next player he recommended, sight unseen.

Towe was that player, and it was a decision that Sloan never regretted, adopting Towe as a coaching extension on the floor during his college career and welcoming Towe back to N.C. State as an assistant coach when Towe's brief professional career ended.

"Monte we signed without hardly doing anything," says Sam Esposito, one of Sloan's assistants at the time and the Wolfpack's head baseball coach who frequently recruited Indiana for the Wolfpack. "I had another kid from Indiana (Hill) who was a bullet, a small guy like Monte, but he changed his mind and ended up going somewhere else. That is one of the reasons we ended up taking Monte. We never thought he was going to be the player that he was."

Things turned out all right for both Hill and Ahlfeld, as well. Hill is in his third term as the U.S. Congressman from Indiana's 9th District and is a member with Towe in the Indiana Basketball Hall of Fame. Ahlfeld ended up going to Indiana as one of Bobby Knight's first recruits, helping the Hoosiers win three consecutive Big Ten championships before going on to medical school. He's now the team orthopedic surgeon for his alma mater.

Towe had long wanted to go to Purdue, as his older brothers and sisters did, but the Boilermakers weren't interested. In fact, Bradley University and a couple of other Midwestern mid-majors were the only schools that showed even the slightest interest in Towe.

So when N.C. State, a school well-known to most Indiana high school players because of Sloan's ties to Indiana and Hoosier legend Everett Case, came calling, Towe jumped at the chance, even if he wasn't considered to be the best of the seven freshman recruits.

"Like always, all I ever wanted was a chance to show I could play," says Towe, who has been the head coach at the University of New Orleans since 2001.

Sloan was sure that Towe would get killed on the defensive end, and that may

AP/WWP

have been true had there not been a pair of safety nets named Thompson and Burleson. Thompson managed to help pick up any stray guards coming into the lane with sheer athletic ability; Burleson was simply too big to shoot over for smaller guards.

Besides, no matter who Towe was paired with during early scrimmages in his freshman year, whether he worked with Thompson or with Burleson or with Stoddard, his team usually won, thanks to Towe's bulldog spirit.

"We would scrimmage against the varsity, and as Coach Esposito remembers it, my team would always win," Towe says. "I would be matched with Tommy, and we would win. I would be matched with David, and we would win. That kind of got their attention."

Eventually, the mountainous Burleson and the tiny Towe caught the attention of the college basketball world, as the long-and-the-short-of-it roommates who played with Thompson. The school, for a while, liked to promote Towe as 5-7 and Burleson as 7-5, though neither was particularly accurate. Towe was more in the neighborhood of five foot five—in his bare feet, while Burleson, when measured for the NBA, topped out at seven foot two.

Towe was always quick to point out he always wore shoes when he played, so he went with the more liberal five-foot-seven measurement.

By the time Towe and Thompson became eligible as sophomores, they both contributed immediately, with Towe stepping in at point guard and Joe Cafferky moving to the other guard position. Sloan could barely drag Towe off the court, even when

wearing a cast to protect his broken left wrist or a mask to protect the broken nose he suffered against Virginia his sophomore year.

Sloan never forgot the raspy voice he heard from the end of the bench that night about 10 minutes after Towe had his nose broken by Wally Walker.

"I turned to tell him something and there were tears running down his face," Sloan said in a 1974 interview with the *Basketball Times*. "The trainer said it was OK, so I told him to go in. He was out there as usual, diving for balls, scraing for steals and making life miserable. In Monte's own mind, he had to prove to himself, to his teammates and to the fans that he was all right."

Towe was in the starting lineup from the minute he became eligible as a sophomore, and led the Wolfpack in assists three consecutive years. It was clear, as Esposito always said, Towe was the guy who made the Wolfpack go.

"Nobody could press him," Thompson says. "I often heard (North Carolina coach) Dean Smith talk about the guy who was the biggest problem for them and he didn't say it was me or Tommy. He said it was Monte, because they couldn't really use the defenses they wanted to against us because Monte was so quick. After that, they really couldn't press us, because we would make them pay at the other end, with an easy layup.

"Monte was a tough guard, and the fact that he was so tough with the ball, it made it hard to apply a lot of different defenses and apply a lot of pressure that other teams wanted to."

Burleson also benefited from Towe's ability to pull up short in the offense and drain many 25-footers, shots that would easily be beyond the three-point line in today's game.

"A lot of guys today play footsy with that line," says Burleson. "But Monte's shot would be four or five feet behind it. He would always let it go from 22 feet, and he would hit the shot. That was critical for me, because if those guys on the perimeter can't hit the shot, then the defense collapses inside and jams up the middle for me, and I wouldn't have been able to do what I needed to do.

"He was the perfect point guard who could break a press, make his shot, make good passes and always make the appropriate play. And he was money on the free throw line."

Fast money, in fact. No one in ACC history ever had a quicker release on his free throws than Towe. *The Charlotte Observer* once put a stopwatch on Towe's release after he received the ball from the game official, and timed it at less than a second. Towe remembers a game in the old Charlotte Coliseum, when the official handed him the ball, turned briefly to the scorer's table, then looked back at Towe and said: "OK, Monte, you can shoot."

Towe had already made the free throw and was waiting for the ball for his second shot.

"I always shot the ball that way, going back to when I was Indiana growing up," Towe says. "It probably came from my own impatience. I would always have to make 10 free throws in a row before I went to bed at night. I would shoot them quickly so I could get inside, and I ended up turning that practice form into my game form."

Towe's ability to throw the pass also helped invent one of basketball's most artistic and acrobatic plays—the alley-oop pass. One day in practice during his freshman season, Towe misfired on a pass to Thompson, who was coming at the rim from the baseline. The ball was way high, far out of even Thompson's reach.

So everyone thought.

The leaping forward with the 44-inch vertical jump went up and got the ball and laid it in the basket as he came down.

"You know, that's a pretty good play," Sloan said after seeing Thompson score the basket. "Let's use that from now on."

Both Towe and Stoddard, who went on to have a 15-year major league baseball career, became masters at lobbing the ball up to Thompson, who managed to catch the ball and lay it in without dunking, which at the time was against NCAA rules.

"That was a different type of art form," Towe says, "but David was a master of catching the ball and laying it in."

Towe was the key figure in guiding the Wolfpack to its '74 championship, motivating the sometimes dovish Thompson and the sporadically hawkish Burleson. Against UCLA in the semifinals, Towe made the play that shifted momentum in the second overtime. With the Wolfpack trailing by seven points with just over two minutes to play, Towe stepped in front of the Bruins' All-America center Bill Walton to draw a charge. He later made the game-clinching free throws that ended UCLA's seven-year reign as national champions.

"It was all like a fairytale.
And we rode it to the max."

In the anticlimactic championship game against Marquette, Towe poured in 16 points, second only to Thompson's 21 in the title game.

"Don't talk to me about Thompson and Burleson," Marquette coach Al McGuire said after the title game. "The key to their team is the little white kid in the backcourt. We like to think our guards are quick on defense, but he kept buzzing past them like they were standing still."

As in high school, Towe was more than just a basketball player. He spent three years playing second base for Esposito on the Wolfpack baseball team, joining with Stoddard in leading the Wolfpack to the first three ACC baseball championships.

He still remembers the excitement of the 1974 ACC title, though not the one played at Greensboro Coliseum. Third baseman Ronnie Evans hit the game-winning home run late in the game, and Towe remembers Thompson jumping over the fence—not even a very high hurdle, really—to meet Evans at the plate.

Towe came back to coach under Sloan, when Eddie Biedenbach became the head coach at Davidson. He followed Sloan to Florida and was in line to succeed his mentor

until Sloan was forced to resign as the Gators head coach on Halloween, 1990. Towe wandered from several jobs, including the head coach and general manager of the Raleigh Bullfrogs of the Global Basketball Association and an assistant position with Biedenbach at UNC-Asheville before finally becoming a head coach for two years at Santa Fe Community College in Gainesville, Florida. He was hired at New Orleans in 2001, and given a five-year contract extension in 2004.

For a little guy who most never gave a chance of playing college basketball, Towe will never forget his experiences of knocking off college basketball's biggest giant and winning N.C. State's first national championship.

"It was all like a fairytale," Towe said. "And we rode it to the max."

The year 2002 was big in honoring the little point guard. He was inducted into the Indiana Basketball Hall of Fame, joining Everett Case, Norm Sloan and Vic Bubas. That was also the year N.C. State made Towe's No. 25 jersey one of the few that hangs in the rafters of the RBC Center.

You know what? It hangs just as tall as all the others.

KENNY CARR

How could Kenny Carr not want to be part of this? Carr was sitting in Reynolds Coliseum that weekend in March 1974, when the Wolfpack hosted the Eastern Regionals of the NCAA Tournament. Fresh off the most memorable game in ACC Tournament history, the Wolfpack played Providence and Pittsburgh in the first two rounds of the tournament, and Carr, a senior at DeMatha High School, was visiting to see if he might want to make Raleigh his college basketball home.

He watched the Wolfpack pummel Providence in that first game, then two days later sat in horror with the rest of the 12,400 people at Reynolds Coliseum when David Thompson tripped over Phil Spence's shoulder, fell to the ground and lay lifeless on the floor.

But when Thompson came back from the hospital in the second half, the building erupted in its loudest celebration ever, and Carr knew he wanted to play at N.C. State.

"I got caught up in the hoopla," he says.

As a kid, Carr was a football player. That's what he did growing up in Washington, D.C., and it might have been a good sport for the physical, hard-working athlete to pursue, with his eventual size and determination. But one day, all the kids on the playground stopped playing football, and walked over to some nearby basketball courts. It was a game that the 14-year-old Kenny had never really tried.

He was hooked in seconds.

"It was kind of by accident, to be honest, but I just fell in love with basketball," he says. "Plus, back in those days, it was kind of tough to find football shoes that would fit

KENNY CARR

Born: August 15, 1955 (Washington, D.C.)
High School: DeMatha Catholic High School, Hyattsville, Maryland
Degree: B.S. Education, N.C. State, 1980
Position: Forward
Number: 32 (honored)
Years with the Wolfpack: 1974-77
Honors:
★ President, Carr Construction, Portland, Ore.
★ Led ACC in scoring in 1976 at 26.6 points per game and '77 at 21.0 points per game
★ 1975, '77 First-team All-ACC Tournament
★ 1976, '77 First-team All-ACC selection
★ 1976 Olympic team (gold medal)
★ 1976 and '77 ACC scoring leader
★ 1976 and '77 All-ACC selection
★ 1977 NBA first-round pick (Los Angeles Lakers, sixth overall pick)
★ 1998 Inductee in to DeMatha High School Hall of Fame

me, to tell the truth. That was one of the reasons I didn't want to play."

Nowadays, Carr doesn't have any trouble finding shoes to fit, since he lives in Oregon, right in the shadow of the world's largest athletic shoe company. But then, basketball was a way to make his size-14 feet more comfortable. Plus, he got to play most of his games indoors.

Carr, a six-foot, eight-inch forward, spent three years scoring and rebounding for Wolfpack Coach Norm Sloan in the days immediately following the 1974 NCAA Championship. Though the two-time All-American never got to play in the NCAA Tournament, he did spend one year playing with David Thompson, then inherited Thompson's crown as a multiple ACC scoring leader.

> # "Kenny Carr ended up being a truly great college player. He was one of the toughest, strongest forwards ever. I'm not sure people really ever appreciated him, and what he accomplished."
>
> [EDDIE BIEDENBACH]

Thompson led the league three consecutive years from 1973-75, and Carr won the league scoring titles in 1976 and '77, averaging 26.6 and 21.0 points per game, respectively. That gave N.C. State five unbroken years with the league's top scorer, a stretch that has never been equaled in more than a half century of play in the Atlantic Coast Conference.

But Carr, who scored at least 30 points nine times in his college career, wasn't just a scoring machine. Even though he played in just 86 games, he is still ranked among the best rebounders in school history.

"Kenny was a great, great player," said longtime N.C. State sports information director Frank Weedon. "But he was so stoic and never showed any emotions, and I think people forget about him. He may have been the second greatest player to ever play here, behind David."

Carr ended up at N.C. State because of assistant coach Eddie Biedenbach's persistence in pursuing DeMatha star Adrian Dantley, who eventually ended up at Notre Dame. One day during Dantley's senior season, Biedenbach was watching the team practice, when DeMatha coach Morgan Wootten

mentioned that he might want to watch someone else on the court.

"You see Kenny Carr right there," Wootten told Biedenbach. "You will be working just as hard for him as you are for Adrian Dantley right now."

That gave Biedenbach a head start in wooing Carr, who flew a bit under the radar as a junior because of a knee injury he suffered the year before. He favored it for an entire year, Biedenbach says, so other recruiters didn't take much notice.

"Then, his senior year, he just exploded," Biedenbach says. "I had a heads up on everybody because of recruiting Dantley and sitting there with Morgan. I think they gave me an honorary degree for the number of hours I spent up there for two years.

"Kenny Carr ended up being a truly great college player. He was one of the toughest, strongest forwards ever. I'm not sure people really ever appreciated him, and what he accomplished."

Carr holds several distinctions in the decorated annals of Wolfpack basketball: He forged the path for other Wootten-coached DeMatha High School players to find N.C.

Chris Seward/*Technician*

State, which led to Sidney Lowe and Dereck Whittenburg (among many others) playing for the Wolfpack; he and Tommy Burleson are the only two N.C. State players to ever play for the U.S. Olympic team (Tom Gugliotta was selected for the 2000 team, but was hurt and never played); Carr in fact is the only Wolfpack player to ever win Olympic gold; and Carr is the first N.C. State basketball player to leave early for the NBA, an opportunity that Thompson passed up in 1974.

Carr, whose honored No. 32 jersey hangs from the rafters of the RBC Center, will always be linked to Thompson because of their five-year scoring streak, and because Carr was the school's first superstar after Thompson, a rather unenviable position primarily because Carr was such a different kind of player: a big, strong, aggressive forward who liked to step outside and take jump shots.

"To me, Kenny was one of those players that was ahead of his time," said former North Carolina rival and Olympic teammate Phil Ford. "Now, it's not uncommon to see someone with Kenny's size and strength with the ability to play on the perimeter and knock in jump shots or put the ball on the deck and drive to the basket. When we were coming along, guys with Kenny's strength and size always played inside. He was just a little before his time."

Ford remembers seeing the awe in the eyes of the Spanish national team during an exhibition game before the Olympics in Montreal, as they watched Carr take over the scrimmage with the authority of a CEO, which is in fact what Carr became.

"That was not my forte, running a mile. It was a mental thing. I just hated it."

[KENNY CARR]

The Olympic experience was perhaps the biggest moment of Carr's career. After the 1972 team lost in the controversial game to the Russians, the 1976 team was determined to get the gold medal back, and North Carolina coach Dean Smith was given the task of doing it. He held tryouts on N.C. State's campus, and Carr was one of the 15 finalists.

Smith required that all his players could run a mile under a certain time, and Carr missed that time badly on his first attempt. Had Indiana's Quinn Buckner not helped pace Carr on his second attempt, he may not have been one of the team's 12 members, joining Dantley of Notre Dame, plus Buckner, Ford, Indiana's Scott May and North Carolina's Mitch Kupchak, Tommy LaGarde and Walter Davis.

"That was not my forte, running a mile," Carr says, laughing. "It was a mental thing. I just hated it."

He loved the Olympic experience, not so much the Games in Montreal, where the Americans won all of their games to win back the gold medal. Carr averaged 6.8 points and 3.2 rebounds in six games. It was more the tryouts, the practices and the exhibition tour around the country that were even more fun.

"I just enjoyed throwing the ball up with some of the best players in the world," Carr says. "The best competition we had was in training camp. I think the best time of the whole thing was when we were in Chapel Hill and we would just get up and play every day. That is the most fun I have ever had."

Besides, the accommodations in Montreal weren't all that great. The 12 players on the team shared a single two-bedroom, one-bath condominium in the Olympic Village, a far cry from the luxurious digs that the modern-day Dream Team players require. Carr believes that 1976 team should be remembered.

"As far as I am concerned, our team won the last legitimate gold medal there was for the United States," Carr said. "In 1980, we boycotted Russia. In 1984, they boycotted us. In 1988, we lost it (to Yugoslavia). And in 1992, we started the Dream Team."

Carr came back from the Olympics with a pretty good idea that he would only spend one more year in college, an idea he got from former Maryland player Brad Davis.

"I just thought my body and my game was ready to move on," Carr says. "I was a very physical player, and I would get a lot of fouls. I was a little bigger and more aggressive than most people I played against. I got frustrated, and I figured it was time to move on."

"As far as I am concerned, our team won the last legitimate gold medal there was for the United States. In 1980, we boycotted Russia. In 1984, they boycotted us. In 1988, we lost it (to Yugoslavia). And in 1992, we started the Dream Team."

[KENNY CARR]

He was the sixth overall pick in the 1977 NBA draft, going to the Los Angeles Lakers. His career got off to a rocky start after he broke his right foot in his rookie season and his left foot in his second season. But he still played for 10 years with four different franchises (Los Angeles, Cleveland, Portland and Detroit), retiring in 1987 after 674 games, 7,713 points and 4,999 rebounds.

He eventually settled down in Portland, where he stumbled on another unexpected career path. In 1982, he bought a 50-year-old, 6,000-square-foot home that needed extensive renovation. The final bill came out to be $250,000.

"Gosh," he thought, "there has got to be some profit in this."

Carr became a general contractor, a bit of a departure from the Education degree he earned from N.C. State. Even though Carr left school early, he returned the summer after his junior year for two summer school sessions, then took the final class he needed to graduate during his rookie year with the Los Angeles Lakers.

After weathering a couple of Northwest economic slowdowns, Carr got into specialty contracting, fabricating and erecting structural steel for commercial and industrial projects. In 2003, Carr Construction Co. had about 120 employees and did $23 million in business in the Portland area.

Carr, who celebrated his 25th anniversary with wife Adrianna in 2004, had always intended to return to his hometown of Washington, D.C., but the success of his business and the arrival of his three kids—Cameron, Devon and Alyx—rooted him in the Northwest.

"My kids liked being here, and we were settled," Carr says. "Once that happens, you don't necessarily live your life for yourself anymore. You make compromises."

Carr had made plenty of compromises earlier in his life, switching from football to basketball, leaving school for his professional career, getting into an unlikely post-basketball profession.

But, as his jersey hangs in the rafters of the RBC Center, Carr will always be remembered as the Wolfpack star that blossomed immediately after Thompson.

"My kids liked being here, and we were settled. Once that happens, you don't necessarily live your life for yourself anymore. You make compromises."

[KENNY CARR]

N.C. State Student Media Authority/*Technician*

JIM
VALVANO

Jim Valvano may have had an inkling, standing in that cramped little room at the Meadowlands, that he had just seen his last chance of winning a national championship ruined by a call so awful that it turned a veteran ACC official into the Wolfpack nation's version of Bill Buckner.

"Christ!" Valvano would say later that night. "It was all right there in front of us."

It was March, 1989, and Valvano was absolutely positive that the only Wolfpack team he led to an ACC regular-season championship had the special qualities needed to win another national championship. The combination of senior forward Chucky Brown, unheralded junior Brian Howard, plus the sophomore version of "Fire & Ice," Chris Corchiani and Rodney Monroe, and a couple of young big men was hardly a great team. But it had developed a chemistry that rivaled the 1983 trio of Dereck Whittenburg, Sidney Lowe and Thurl Bailey that made Valvano famous.

"We just played so well together," Corchiani says. "Because we had been through so much together."

Under the shadow of controversy caused by the announced publication of a tell-all book about unseemly practices in Valvano's program, the Wolfpack won 10 ACC games and finished first in the regular-season standings, the only time that has happened since the 1974 team won the national championship.

When Valvano's team bowed out of the ACC Tournament in the first round, becoming the first top seed to ever lose to a No. 8 seed, it appeared that any kind of real run in the NCAA Tournament would not happen.

But the Wolfpack steamrolled South Carolina in the first round and outlasted Iowa in a double-overtime game in Providence, Rhode Island. And, with three minutes to play, State trailed top-seeded and second-ranked Georgetown by a mere three points, after coming all the way back from a 16-point second-half deficit.

Corchiani pulled up for a short jump-shot in the lane, over the outstretched arms of Georgetown freshman Alonzo Mourning, who had played poorly and was in deep foul trouble. The ball went in, the whistle blew,

"On the record, I think it was an unfortunate call."

[JIM VALVANO]

and it appeared that Corchiani was headed to the foul line for a game-tying free throw and Mourning was headed to the bench with his fifth foul.

But Rick Hartzell, a veteran ACC referee who was standing in front of the Hoya bench, hesitated for a second before calling the foul. Then he began rolling his arms around to indicate a traveling call on Corchiani. Hartzell waved off the basket and gave the ball to the Hoyas, all but ending the comeback and any chance the Wolfpack had of playing ACC rival Duke in the East Region finals for a chance to go to the Final Four.

At the time, CBS analyst Billy Packer called it "the worst call in the history of the NCAA Tournament."

Following the game, Hartzell jumped over the Georgetown bench and headed for the officials' locker room. Valvano seethed in silence for most of the night. The party line from everyone after the game was that "it was an unfortunate call." Valvano must have said it two dozen times in his postgame press conference. Every player on the team used the exact same phrase when asked about what happened. Anyone looking into State's program for a conspiracy would have found one right there.

Finally, long after the morning newspaper reporters had gone to the media work room to file stories, Valvano sat in a small interview room with a couple of big-time buddies—Mike Fratello, Mike Lupica and Tony Kornheiser, among others—and a pair of small-time afternoon reporters from North Carolina: Caulton Tudor of the *The Raleigh Times*, and me, then of *The Salisbury Post*.

Lupica finally tired of the unimaginative company line and said: "Enough of this 'unfortunate call' bull****.' Tell us what you really think."

"On the record," said Valvano, getting wound up for the performance of a lifetime, "I think it was an unfortunate call.

"But off the record... Off the record... Is that thing off?" he said, pointing at the tape recorder in my hand. "Off the record, that was the most chicken**** call I have ever seen. Gutless. He comes running in from right in front of the Georgetown bench, and he makes that call. We were right there, all ready to play Duke. We can take Duke. Our kids know we can take Duke. It was horse****.

"It was all right there. I've felt it all week. We had a perfect plan to beat Georgetown and my kids fought back and pulled it off. Then this chicken**** mother****** makes that call. It was all in place. We could win another one.

"And this guy. Jesus Christ, he's one of our own guys. I'm going to have to call up my

Uncle Guido and have him take care of him. Sonofa*****. It was the most gutless, chicken**** thing I ever saw.

"But on the record—on the record—it was an unfortunate call."

It was the perfect Valvano moment—hilarious, competitive, a little violent and a little arrogant—staged perfectly in front of the media that built his legend.

In a seven-minute, profanity-laced tirade—he was as good at those as he was telling a funny joke—Valvano let off all the steam that had been building for three months, following the release of a book jacket cover that eventually forced the multiple public and private investigations that led to his resignation from the school at the end of the following season.

In his heart, Valvano might have known that it wasn't Hartzell's fault. The Wolfpack had been down 42-28 at the half, and trailed the whole game. At least that's what Valvano told Hartzell when the two ran across each other in the Raleigh-Durham International Airport only a few months before Valvano died of cancer in 1993.

"Was it a bad call?" Hartzell says 15 years after the fact. "Yeah, it probably was. But I have purposefully never watched the tape. To his credit, Jim always said that the call didn't cost him the game, that there had probably been a half-dozen other calls in the first half that went the other way, and it all evens out.

"I saw him near the end, walking through the airport in Raleigh, and I went over to talk to him. We laughed, we hugged, and I made peace with it. I know he made peace with it, too."

That's the thing about Valvano, more than two decades after he led the Wolfpack on its exciting three-week ride to the 1983 NCAA championship and 10 years after his untimely death at the age of 47. Most people have now made their peace with him, and what remains is a legacy of devoted supporters and fans that remember the good he brought to the university in his 10 years of service as basketball coach, and for four years, athletics director.

But 18 months of acrimonious scrutiny by the NCAA and local and national media, as allegations of academic and drug-testing fraud and point-shaving and gambling scandals raged around him, ended with Valvano being forced to step aside from his job for life. Do you think Valvano was bitter? He titled his autobiography *They Gave Me a Lifetime Contract, and Then They Declared Me Dead*. Both he and his family believe the stress brought on by the dogged pursuit of many allegations had something to do with the onslaught of cancer that took his life on April 28, 1993.

That was only months after Valvano, ever the motivational speaker even when he had to have his friends carry him on stage, gave two inspirational performances, in which he made the phrase "Don't give up, don't ever give up" a rallying cry in both athletics and cancer research. Valvano never did up, but he couldn't fight off the ravages of a superior opponent.

He is remembered now by his players and college basketball fans for the inspiration and legacy that still fights and competes more than a decade after the coach himself was buried. The Jimmy V Foundation, based

"I can flat out tell you, his legacy to me is not cutting down the nets in 1983 or winning the national title, but it is the millions and millions of dollars that have been raised through the Jimmy V Foundation."

[DICK VITALE]

in Cary, North Carolina, has raised more than $32 million since Valvano's death and given out millions in grants for cancer research. It looks to be a lasting memory for a coach who inspired one of the most memorable championship games in NCAA Tournament history. Could the father of the Cardiac Pack really one day help cure cancer? That's the primary goal of a well-funded organization that includes a powerful Board of Directors and a touch of Valvano's extended family.

"I can flat out tell you, his legacy to me is not cutting down the nets in 1983 or winning the national title, but it is the millions and millions of dollars that have been raised through the Jimmy V Foundation," says Dick Vitale, Valvano's one-time television partner and a member of the foundation's board, along with such personalities as Mike Krzyzewski, Bill Cosby, Phil Knight and Kay Yow. "To me, it is just amazing. It is all because of his personality."

But, oy, that's not the way things were in and around Raleigh for nearly two years as Valvano's program imploded around him, and the university went to extremes to make sure it cleansed itself of the perception that athletics was more important on campus than aca-

demics. Perhaps it was inevitable that the fast-talking cannoli from Long Island would be chased out of his comfortable banana puddin' life in Raleigh. From that first spring day when he confused the Greenville in North Carolina with the Greenville in South Carolina, Valvano seemed a little out of place.

"Growing up in New York, I was an Italian," Valvano said in a 1986 interview, just after he came back from Italy. "In Raleigh, I am an EYE-talian. I had to go to Italy to become an American."

In the end, the super-charged scandal that ended Valvano's Wolfpack career cost the school its two most prominent coaches and its chancellor, and plunged the athletics department into a decade-long doldrums that delayed for more than 10 years the long-needed improvements to Carter-Finley Stadium and the construction of a new basketball arena.

Not only did Valvano resign following the 1990 basketball season, following in the footsteps of chancellor Bruce Poulton, but football coach Dick Sheridan became so upset with the school's board of trustees he decided that 1993 would be his final season at the school. Then, in the spring of 1993, Sheridan developed his own health problems, found out he needed surgery that would sideline him for weeks and decided to hasten his departure.

He stepped down June 29, 1993, a date so close to the start of the football season, the school had little choice but to elevate one of Sheridan's assistants. But Sheridan, who developed a close working relationship with Valvano when the latter became athletics director, had no use for the way the school administration handled Valvano's departure. When the trustees refused to let Valvano, then Sheridan, sit before them and respond to allegations being hurled about the athletics department, both coaches knew their time at the school was nearing its end.

"Frankly, that was the beginning of the end for me and North Carolina State, that they would treat someone who had given so much to the university, that they would not let him or me to come before them to answer the allegations," Sheridan says years later. "They were more caught up in perception than reality."

Did Valvano make mistakes? The perception is that he let his pursuit of doing other things distract him from maintaining control of his program. By 1987, Valvano had his hands in so many pots that he didn't have a firm grip on his team. Some friends and former players admit that now, but there are still those who think Valvano's troubles were jealousy and a basic misunderstanding of what he could accomplish.

"Jim was a very talented guy," Sheridan says. "He certainly had the capacity to do a lot of things, where other people might have found it more difficult to do all those things. Personally, I do not feel like he had more to do than he could handle. He had more to do than a lot of people could handle, but that's not the same thing. It took tremendous energy and a lot of talent, and Jim certainly had both. His personality and his wit and his ability to entertain overshadowed the things that he was able to do, both as a coach and an athletics director."

Perhaps Valvano's biggest problem was that he was an optimist in a cynical world. He always read 70 pages a day on some subject, and spent his two-week beach vacation reading everything he could find about a subject he was interested in. One year it was economic theory. The next summer it was Watergate. He always believed if he could give someone a chance, that person would take advantage of every opportunity, as he did at Rutgers University, where he went from walk-on to starter to winner of the school's Senior Athlete of the Year. But, as he brought in a host of talented players who were flawed people, it began to nip at his heels.

"Jimmy's problem at the end, and I discussed it with him many times, is that he started taking chances with too many kids," Vitale says. "He always felt that if you gave a kid an opportunity, gave him a lot of love and attention, things would turn out great. Bottom line, that backfired on him."

Starting with the recruitment of Chris Washburn, a supremely talented, but immature and coddled center from Hickory, North Carolina, Valvano began bringing in players of questionable academic skills and

maturity levels, and then did not maintain oversight of those players once they got to campus. Even Valvano admitted in his book that getting Washburn—who missed most of his freshman season after Valvano suspended him for stealing a stereo from a dorm room, then left school after his sophomore season for the NBA draft—was the beginning of his troubles.

"He tried to treat us like men," says former player Chucky Brown, who was a senior on the 1989 team that nearly beat Georgetown. "Some guys weren't ready to be treated like men. Some of them were still boys. There is nothing wrong with treating us like men, but it might have been his only fault, because some people weren't ready to be treated that way."

So things got out of control. When allegations began flying that N.C. State was paying its players millions of dollars, that there was rampant misuse of the drug testing program, and there was an undercurrent of seediness throughout the basketball program, Valvano himself called in NCAA investigators for a thorough review.

While most allegations were proven false, the NCAA did find instances of players selling school-provided shoes and complimentary game tickets, which resulted in the one-year probation that kept State out of the 1990 NCAA Tournament and made Valvano the third basketball coach in school history to put the basketball program on probation.

"We all did that," says former Wolfpack guard Chris Corchiani. "It wasn't so much selling the shoes, as it was trading it in for other merchandise at a local store. The shoes might be worth $70 and they would give us $40 or $50 credit. We could get a warm-up suit or something. That was going on, I know for a fact, at every school in the area.

"All the things that were being alleged—changing grades, gambling, taking drug tests for other guys, changing grades—I never saw that stuff going on, and it was never proven. Selling tickets, selling sneakers, that stuff went on. But it went on at all the other universities, too."

As investigations into his program progressed, there became a perception that Valvano had a disdain for academics, because of the poor academic records of his recruits and a poor graduation rate. But it is a false perception. Valvano, who earned a master's degree in English, would constantly spout lines of poetry in his postgame press conferences, in the same manner that current Wake Forest basketball coach Skip Prosser does. Valvano's favorite poem was T.S. Eliot's "The Love Song of J. Alfred Prufrock," and his favorite line was "Do I dare eat a peach?"

Valvano always ate the peach. But he somehow forgot about the pit.

He was one of the most complex people who ever came through the doors of Reynolds Coliseum and Case Athletics Center. He was also extremely smart and extremely talented. In the final four minutes of a close game, he could beat any coach in college or professional basketball. I still have, somewhere in the musty bookshelves of my dad's basement, some of the notebooks Valvano snatched out of my hands in postgame interviews to draw up an explanation

"I always thought he could be the star of a sitcom."

[DICK VITALE]

of a game's decisive play. They almost always worked, with the possible exception of that Georgetown game in 1989, one of the few times the stars didn't align perfectly for the coach.

The Queens-born, Long Island-raised coach could make anybody laugh, be it a professional comedian like Bill Cosby or the leader of the free world like Ronald Reagan. He and Vitale appeared in an episode of *The Cosby Show*, the spoils of a bet they made with Cosby about the fate of Temple in the 1991 NCAA Tournament. During dinner after the show wrapped, Valvano had Cosby on the floor laughing. Following the 1983 championship, Valvano met Ronald Reagan twice at the White House. When Reagan said, "I've always wondered, is it pronounced 'Val-VAHN-o' or 'Val-VANE-o?'" The coach shot back, "And I have always wondered, is it 'REE-gun' or 'RAY-gun?'" He even made priggish North Carolina coach Dean Smith laugh by stealing the ball out of a manager's hands and making a layup immediately after the Tar Heels beat N.C. State in the last men's game ever played in UNC's Carmichael Auditorium. One of my favorite jokes among the many he told on the Wolfpack Club's annual rubber-chicken-and-barbecue tour of the state had to do with his long-suffering wife, Pam. "I went

home one night and told Pam that the NCAA had changed recruiting rules, and that all coaches had to stay on campus and at home for 30 consecutive nights during the summer. My wife looked at me and said, 'Honey, I want to make love 30 straight nights.' I said, 'OK, put me down for two.'"

"I always thought he could be the star of a sitcom," Vitale says.

In fact, that was part of the discussions when UCLA courted Valvano in 1988.

I did see Valvano awed once, completely too shy to speak. I was a reporter, just out of school, at *The Salisbury Post*, a small afternoon paper in the pretty little town between Greensboro and Charlotte that is home to the National Sportscasters and Sportswriters Hall of Fame. In the summer of 1988, Bob Costas organized an all-star baseball game between his television buddies and the Catawba College baseball team at Newman Park, a rickety old minor league stadium on the edge of town. Costas, who carried that Mickey Mantle rookie card in his wallet for so long, brought in Valvano, Paul Maguire, Bucky Waters and a handful of you-gotta-be-kidding fill-ins like gymnast Bart Conner and the Late Night with David Letterman writer who played Flunky the Clown to play for his team. They were all outfitted in throw-back

> # "He didn't hide much of anything. His style, as an outward, Italian guy, in Raleigh, North Carolina, it was different. I thought he was refreshing. I thought he was amazing, and I loved him."
>
> [MIKE KRZYZEWSKI]

Washington Senators' uniforms. The big draw, however, was that Mantle showed up that day to sign autographs.

Valvano, a Yankees fan who liked to argue the relative merits of Mantle over Joe DiMaggio with his father, played shortstop in the field and did not get a hit in the game. In his first at-bat, he walked on four straight pitches—he bribed the umpire before the game—and was pulled for a pinch runner, an NBC producer named Lisa Stern. But every time Valvano came off the field, he would go sit next to Mantle, unable to crack a joke, silenced by the proximity of his hero.

But heroes fall. Mantle left Newman Park that afternoon after the sixth inning, went to the local Shoney's for an all-you-can-eat buffet, got into a shouting match with another patron and was asked to leave for creating a disturbance.

Valvano's downfall came after he ate too long from the buffet, when he became more of an enterprise—JTV Enterprises, in fact—than a basketball coach. He dabbled in a little of everything, from advertising to television hosting to motivational speaking to athletics administration. By 1986, *USA Today*

listed him as the nation's highest paid basketball coach, making about $750,000 a year, from his university salary, his television and radio deals, his shoe contract, his motivational speaking and all his other outside sources.

When Vitale brought that up to him in a television interview, Valvano turned it into a joke. "That was a couple of years ago, Dick," Valvano said. "If you are going to ask me about it, at least get the numbers right."

He was the forerunner of the multimillionaire coaches of today, for whom all those sources of income are a simple byproduct of being the head coach of a major basketball program. There's hardly any scandal associated with it at all now.

"He didn't hide it," says Krzyzewski, who competed against Valvano as a player and a coach, then developed a close friendship while Valvano was receiving treatments at Duke Medical Center. "He didn't hide much of anything. His style, as an outward, Italian guy, in Raleigh, North Carolina, it was different. I thought he was refreshing. I thought he was amazing, and I loved him. He was threatening, he was different and sometimes he got a number of bad things said about him. I don't think it was warranted."

When Valvano's income became public knowledge, it added to a boiling fury on campus, where the academic side of the university was still upset that the school had been denied, for the fourth time, a bid to join the prestigious Phi Beta Kappa honor society. During the 1985 national convention, a Duke professor stood up and denounced N.C. State's bid, based mainly on the poor academic performance of the men's basketball team.

In the end, the resignation of Poulton, Valvano's biggest supporter outside the athletics department, spelled the end of Valvano's tenure. When allegations of more academic abuses by former director of State's tutoring program, Hugh Fuller, came out, Valvano finally agreed to a negotiated settlement and resignation following the 1990 season.

Did Valvano make mistakes? Of course, and it tarnished his legacy. He allowed an atmosphere to surround his program that made all of the allegations believable, even those that proved to be untrue.

"When I first heard all the things that were being said, I thought it would go away," says Corchiani, who settled back in Raleigh after spending more than 10 years playing basketball professionally in Europe. "But before you knew it, it got momentum and kept building and building. We certainly did have some characters on the team that when you heard the allegations and you saw the people and you started putting the pieces of the puzzle together, it wasn't the most far-fetched thing I had ever heard.

"To me, if V was here, if he could go back and do things over, that was one of the things he would do differently. He just gave these young kids way too much freedom. We didn't have curfews. It wasn't as structured as it should have been. The game now is such a high-dollar industry, these are kids, these are not grown men. You have got to monitor them. You depend on them. If one of them is out of line, it jumps up and slaps you in the face."

"Time heals all wounds. I would hope that we are moving forward again."

There's no question that, because of the Jimmy V Foundation and the millions it has raised for cancer research, much of the tarnish on Valvano's tenure at N.C. State has been polished away and his sullied image has been rehabilitated.

His tuxedoed speech at the ESPY's just before he died, which was similar in theme to the one he gave at Reynolds Coliseum in celebration of the 10-year anniversary of the 1983 championship, keeps his dream of finding a cure for cancer alive. In the same way, Valvano's 1983 miracle run that ended with Lorenzo Charles's famous game-winning dunk keeps alive the dream of every Cinderella team that ever lived on the NCAA Tournament bubble.

And those two things, above all, would make Valvano smile.

DERECK WHITTENBURG

SIDNEY LOWE

THURL BAILEY

There was a little soft spot on the old wooden floor of Reynolds Coliseum, before it was cut up and sold to fans as souvenirs. It was over on the wing, beyond the top of the key, just a few feet from where the men's basketball team sat for 50 years.

Only Dereck Whittenburg knows exactly where it was. And every time he walks into the hallowed old gym, he picks up a basketball, goes right to that place and pulls up for a still-sweet jumper.

"I always want to hit the shot," Whittenburg says. "That's a special spot."

That's where the miracle began.

From that little square of hardwood, on January 12, 1983, Whittenburg went up for a jumper, crashed through the floor, flew through the basement and landed in the worst possible depths of Hell.

At least that's how it seemed at the time.

What actually happened was, Whittenburg landed on Virginia guard Othell Wilson's foot, breaking the same fifth metatarsal in his right foot that he had during his sophomore year at DeMatha High School. The initial prognosis, after X-rays at Rex Hospital, was that the injury would need at least eight weeks to heal.

Team doctors were almost certain that the senior guard's Wolfpack career was over.

When Coach Jim Valvano, hidden in a private room in the depths of the Reynolds basement, heard the news, he kicked the door and cursed his captain's—and his team's—horrible luck. How would he know that he had just won a national championship?

That was the singular moment that inspired what happened over the next three

DERECK WHITTENBURG

Born: October 2, 1960 (Glenarden, Maryland)
High School: DeMatha Catholic High School, Hyattsville, Maryland
Degree: B.A., Management, 1984
Position: Shooting guard, assistant coach
Number: 25 (honored)
Years with the Wolfpack: 1980-83 (player), 1988-90 (assistant coach)
NCAA Tournament Appearances: 1980, '82, '83
Championships: 1983 ACC Championship; 1983 NCAA Championship
Honors:
★ Second in school history with 47.6 3-point shooting percentage
★ 1979 McDonald's All-American
★ 1982 Second-team All-ACC selection
★ 1982 Second-team All-ACC Tournament
★ 1983 First-team All-ACC Tournament
★ 1983 All-Final Four team
★ Head coach, Wagner University (1999-2003), Fordham University (2003-present)
★ 1983 NBA third-round draft pick (Phoenix Suns, 51st overall pick)
★ DeMatha Catholic High Athletics Hall of Fame
★ Board of Directors, Jimmy V Foundation

SIDNEY LOWE

Born: January 21, 1960 (Washington, D.C.)
High School: DeMatha Catholic High School, Hyattsville, Maryland
Degree: B.S., Mechanical Engineering, N.C. State, 1983
Position: Point guard
Number: 35 (honored)
Years with the Wolfpack: 1980-83
NCAA Tournament Appearances: 1980, '82, '83
Championships: 1983 ACC Championship, 1983 NCAA Championship
Honors:
★ Second in school history with 762 career assists
★ Led ACC in 1981 at 7.7 assists per game, in '83 at 7.5 assists per game

- ★ Third in school history with 220 steals
- ★ Led ACC in 1981 with 2.4 steals per game
- ★ 1979 McDonald's All-American
- ★ 1981 Second-team All-ACC selection
- ★ 1983 First-team All-ACC selection
- ★ 1983 First-team All-ACC Tournament
- ★ 1983 Winner of Everett Case Award (ACC Tournament Most Valuable Player)
- ★ 1983 All-Final Four team
- ★ 1983 Jon Speaks Award winner
- ★ Head coach of Vancouver/Memphis Grizzlies, 2000-02
- ★ DeMatha High School Athletics Hall of Fame

THURL BAILEY

Born: April 7, 1961 (Washington, D.C.)
High School: Bladensburg High School, Bladensburg, Maryland
Degree: B.A., Speech Communications, 1983
Position: Power forward
Number: 41 (honored)
Years with the Wolfpack: 1980-83
NCAA Tournament Appearances: 1980, '82, '83
Championships: 1983 ACC Championship; 1983 NCAA Championship
Honors:
- ★ Owns school record with 207 career blocked shots
- ★ 1982 Second-team All-ACC selection
- ★ 1982 Jon Speaks Award winner
- ★ 1983 First-team All-ACC selection
- ★ 1983 First-team All-ACC Tournament
- ★ 1983 All-Final Four team
- ★ 1983 H.C. Kennett Award winner
- ★ 1983 First-round NBA draft pick (Utah Jazz, seventh overall pick)
- ★ 1979 Bladensburg High School Student Body President
- ★ Founder, Big TLC Foundation
- ★ Chairman, Big T Productions, Fertile Earth, FourLeaf Films
- ★ 2000 Pearl Awards: Best Contemporary Recording, Best New Artist of the Year

months, as Whittenburg and his senior partners with the Wolfpack, Sidney Lowe and Thurl Bailey, helped mold a motley collection of young talent into a Cinderella story that still induces March Madness more than 20 years later.

By losing Whittenburg, the Wolfpack was without its soul. Lowe, the heady point guard, was always the team's brain, an extension of Valvano's coaching tactics on the floor. Bailey, the late-blooming forward, was the team's heart, an emotional leader for whom tears flowed freely.

But Whittenburg, the sweet-shooting guard who had teamed with Lowe even in high school, was the irreplaceable leader, the guy who would take a game-winning shot without blinking, someone who would say, "Let's go, boys," and know that there would be a dozen guys behind him. On that night against Virginia, Whittenburg scored 27 points in the first half, taking his team to unimagined heights against Ralph Sampson and the second-ranked Cavaliers.

Things fell apart, however, after Whittenburg limped off the court and to the locker room, seemingly never to be heard from again. It appeared that the Wolfpack, its organs still intact, wouldn't be able to survive without its soul. That's when Valvano stepped in to deliver the inspirational message that he repeated through a nasty departure from the school and throughout his very public fight with cancer: Don't ever give up.

"Now, a lot of people are writing us off," Valvano told his team the day after Whittenburg's injury. "They are saying our season is over. I'm telling you, I believe something good is going to happen to us. I'm telling you it's too soon to quit."

Valvano sold that dream to his team, as only he could. He made some major adjustments to his style of play, changing from an up-tempo, transition style that took advantage of Whittenburg's and Lowe's shooting abilities to more of a half-court motion game that took advantage of freshman Ernie Myers's ability to slash to the basket.

Early on, the adjustment didn't go well. Including the loss to Virginia, the Wolfpack lost five of its next seven games, entering February with a disappointing 9-7 record. But the improvement wasn't necessarily about wins and losses. It was about maturing and gaining confidence.

"With any team that has a star player, when that player goes down, the other players have to pull together collectively to make up for his absence," says Lorenzo Charles, who was an underutilized sophomore forward at the time. "Dereck's injury allowed some of the role players—Cozell McQueen, Terry Gannon, Alvin Battle, Ernie Myers and me—to more or less grow up and add more to the team. When he came back to the team, it was an added bonus that our fiery leader had come back and was able to help us out through out the season."

Hope was born on February 19, 1983, an unusually warm winter day when defending national champion North Carolina visited Reynolds Coliseum. Valvano had never beaten the Tar Heels since arriving in 1980 and the football team hadn't beaten UNC since 1979. Fans were starting to grumble, even though there seemed to be little chance of a revenue-sport victory in this game, against a team that featured Michael Jordan, Brad Daugherty and Sam Perkins.

But as the clock wound down, Lowe led the Wolfpack down the court on a fast break. Just before he went up for the layup, he bounced the ball between his legs to a trailing Bailey, who completed the play with a thunderous dunk over Perkins. It was a win so significant the players gathered on the court after the game and cut down the nets, rekindling the tradition that Everett Case brought to the school from his days as an Indiana high school legend.

The lasting memory of that moment was of Bailey standing at midcourt, his arms raised high and tears streaming down his face in unbridled joy.

"Nothing has ever made me that emotional," Bailey said at the time. "We had struggled so long and so hard this year, and we deserved a game like that. When the buzzer went off, I closed my eyes and threw my hands in the air. I felt hands tugging on my jersey. I opened my eyes, and I was surrounded. So I surrendered. I was trying to hold back, but I just let the tears go.

"I don't think anything can top that feeling. Even if we went to the NCAA, even to the Final Four, even if we won it all—at that point, at that moment, in that game, I don't think anthing could feel any better than that."

Bailey—and Wolfpack fans everywhere—would soon find out, however, that there was something even better than beating Carolina in a regular-season game at Reynolds Coliseum. Destiny's Darlings were born.

First, Whittenburg came back, exactly 14 games after he broke his foot. It was a

"I don't think anything can top that feeling. Even if we went to the NCAA, even to the Final Four, even if we won it all—at that point, at that moment, in that game, I don't think anything could feel any better than that."

[THURL BAILEY]

remarkably fast recovery, really, similar to the one Whittenburg's first cousin—David Thompson—made in 1974, when he came back from a terrifying fall in the NCAA East Region finals to lead the Wolfpack to its first NCAA championship just a week later.

"I don't know if many people knew this at that time, but I had broken the fifth metatarsal bone before in high school around the same time of the season," Whittenburg says. "I understood what it took to come back. I knew I was coming back, I just didn't know when. The great thing was, the team grew up while I was out. Everybody stepped up their play and they were a better team when I came back."

Second, the role players started to develop. Myers, the flashy freshman from New York, got much of the attention, especially after he scored 35 points against Duke, an ACC record for a first-year player. He averaged 18 points a game and helped the Pack go 9-5 with Whittenburg out of the lineup. Terry Gannon, the sharp-shooter from Joliet, Illinois, never lacked confidence, but Whittenburg's absence

made him an even more important weapon, as he consistently drained shots from beyond the ACC's experimental three-point line. But perhaps the biggest difference came in the maturation of Charles and McQueen, the two inside players who did much of the grunt work while Bailey handled all the post scoring. Forwards Harold Thompson and Alvin Battle also contributed, making the Wolfpack much more capable of having a well-rounded attack instead of being a fast-breaking transition team with guards who could shoot.

Finally, the Wolfpack realized it could win games—big games, like the one against Carolina—with Whittenburg as a leader on the sidelines, not on the court.

What happened in the ACC and NCAA tournaments are both well-chronicled and permanently etched into the minds of Wolfpack fans that lived through that era. The run through the ACC Tournament—with close wins over Wake Forest, North Carolina and Virginia—got the Pack into the NCAA Tournament, and kicked off a party in Raleigh that lasted well into spring.

"It was one of the great stories in the history of our game."

[MIKE KRZYZEWSKI]

Valvano's initial dreams of Whittenburg's return ended with the Wolfpack winning the ACC Championship. He didn't think about the NCAAs, which is why he wasn't sure how his team would do when it opened play against Pepperdine in Corvallis, Oregon.

"We might lose tomorrow night against Pepperdine," Valvano told a group of local reporters covering the team. "It wouldn't surprise me if we do. We're going to be flat as hell. We're going to get caught up in a street brawl with a team that's a lot better than our guys believe, and then we'll get scared and start making stupid mistakes.

"But if we do somehow or other win this game, watch out. I think we'll win it all."

It was a bold prediction, even for a guy who was building his reputation as a master entertainer. Valvano made his career during this month-long run, with the sheer outrageousness of his stand-up routine, the boldness of his confidence and the accuracy of what he said. Everything he said about the Pepperdine game came true. The Wolfpack was wretched but found a way to win the game in double-overtime, even after Lowe fouled out in the first extra period. It found a way to beat Nevada-Las Vegas, Utah, Virginia and Georgia. Houston was the last of the insurmountable obstacles the Wolfpack would face, a game everyone predicted would be won by the team with the most rim-shaking dunks. That's exactly what happened, of course, as the Wolfpack dunked on the first and last basket of the game for the 52-50 victory that still stands as one of the greatest upsets in NCAA Tournament history.

It was a nine-game run that still inspires college teams of lesser talent to believe they too can be national champions. It is one of the reasons today that the NCAA Tournament is second only to the Super Bowl as the nation's greatest sporting event.

"It served as an example for what can be done," says Duke coach Mike Krzyzewski, who has won three national titles in his career. "It set the stage for people to believe a little more the value of a conference tournament. It gave a lot of hope for people in those situations, a reference point. 'Hey, (N.C. State) did it in 1983.'

"It was one of the great stories in the history of our game."

Valvano gets the majority of the credit for his seat-of-the-pants execution that kept opposing coaches guessing and his inspiration. But the three plucky seniors, plus classmate Mike Warren, put the Wolfpack in position to win. They inspired the young guys to grow up after Whittenburg was injured.

They remained the brain, heart and soul of the Cardiac Pack.

"They were our leaders," says Charles, whose game-winning dunk over Houston is a seminal moment in the history of March Madness. "They were the guys we looked up

to. Dereck was our vocal, inspirational leader. There were moments when fatigue set in, and Dereck was the guy who pushed us past that. Dereck was the more energetic of the three seniors.

"Sidney was the leader on the court. We looked to him for instruction probably 95 percent of the game. He was an excellent floor general. Everyone on the team, even Coach V and the rest of the coaching staff, really believed in Sidney.

"Thurl led by example. He worked hard in practice every day. What he did in practice led to production. He was our quiet leader. He just went out there and laid it on the line every night and everyone else just tried to follow. It meant a lot to Thurl. He was a little on the emotional side. That's what basketball should be for a player. You can't just throw on your sneakers and go out there and play. The game has to mean something. It's got to be one of the most important things in the world to you. And it was for Thurl."

All three were successful after they left college. Whittenburg bided his time as an assistant coach on the college level, both under Valvano and Bobby Cremins at Georgia Tech, among others. He got his first head-coaching job at Wagner, where he stayed for three years before becoming the head coach at Fordham in 2003.

Lowe, the ultimate point guard, played four seasons in the NBA for five different teams. He also won three championships while playing in the Continental Basketball Association. He then went from being a coach on the floor to a coach on the bench, spending three years as the head coach of the Vancouver/Memphis Grizzlies. He's now an assistant coach with the Minnesota Timberwolves.

Bailey spent a dozen years playing in the NBA, mostly as a member of the Utah Jazz. He retired in 2001 to become the ultimate Renaissance man: he's a television commentator, motivational speaker and accomplished musician.

But, despite all of their successes, they all say the lasting achievement of their lives was that three-month run to win the NCAA Championship.

"Those moments have been relived a lot over the last 20 years," Bailey said on the day his jersey was honored—along with Lowe's and Whittenburg's, of course—just prior to the 2002-03 season. "Not necessarily by me, but people who always talk to me about it. I wear the championship ring we won most of the time. It's one of those things, that not just to us, but to other people who were involved in it, it was one of the great moments in sports history.

"I had a great NBA career, but somehow people remember that 1983 team. That championship was something special. We were the underdogs, and everybody loves the underdog. People related to what we were doing, and they were riding along with us. I think the whole thing went far beyond sports."

When the plane landed at RDU airport the day after the victory over Houston, the Wolfpack was whisked to Reynolds Coliseum for a raucous extension to the party that had been non-stop on Hillsborough Street from the moment Charles's dunk hit the floor some 2,500 miles away.

As players and coaches and managers stood up to say a few words about the championship, the crowd roared lustily. It was then the Whittenburg got the exact perspective for what he and his soulmates had just pulled off.

"That may have been the first time I realized out of all the hang-ups, out of all the sickness in the world and all the ways people think about how to hurt people..." Whittenburg says, struggling for the right phrasing. "When I saw all those people at Reynolds packed in there, they were all shapes and sizes hugging each other, kissing each other, grabbing each other, chanting and cheering. Some of these were people who otherwise might not even talk to each other on the street.

"I realized that winning in athletics means so much more, because it makes people forget about all the other junk. I thought that was special."

And that's why the lesson learned from that championship, inspired by the three seniors and executed brilliantly by Valvano, is one that will always be relevant.

"They are special, not because they put that banner up there," Valvano said on that February afternoon in 1993, just before he died, in a pregame ceremony honoring the 10th anniversary of the national championship, "but because they taught me, and the world, so many important lessons. No. 1, hope. Things can get better in spite of adversity.

"The '83 team taught us about dreaming, and the importance of dreaming, that nothing can happen, if not first the dream. If you have someone with a dream, a goal and a

Clayton Brinkley/*Technician*

vision, if you have someone who never gives up, who has great hope... That team taught me of persistence, the idea of never, ever quitting."

It's always too soon to quit.

LORENZO
CHARLES

Lorenzo Charles admits it: no one ever got more out of a total screw-up than he did.

There was no reason on that night in Albuquerque, New Mexico, for him to be unattended under the basket. He should have been farther away, like Thurl Bailey was, worrying about boxing out Hakeem Olajuwon, Houston's All-America center. He should have been anywhere except directly under the cylinder, the last place you go for an offensive rebound.

"Most people say I was the guy who was in the right place at the right time," Charles says nearly a quarter century after the most famous put-back in NCAA Tournament history. "Actually, I was in the wrong place at the right time, because as an offensive rebounder, the particular position I was standing in when Dereck (Whittenburg) shot the ball was the wrong place to be.

"I was standing under the cylinder, which is exactly where you don't want to be if you are going to be a decent offensive rebounder."

But in the aftermath of what followed, no one pulled Charles aside to review his rebounding fundamentals. Jim Valvano was too busy looking for someone to hug. The rest of the players were too busy celebrating one of the most unlikely championships in the history of the NCAA Tournament. And everybody back home in Raleigh was too busy storming the Brickyard and Hillsborough Street.

What Charles did that night was purely reactionary. Every time the shot is replayed, he looks like someone who has done something wrong. All he did on the night of

LORENZO CHARLES

Born: November 25, 1963 (Brooklyn, New York)
High School: Brooklyn Tech High School, Brooklyn, New York
Position: Power forward
Number: 43
Years with the Wolfpack: 1981-85
NCAA Tournament Appearances: 1983, '85
Championships: 1983 ACC Championship, 1983 NCAA Championship
Honors:
★ 1983 Second-team All-ACC Tournament
★ 1984, '85 first-team All-ACC selection
★ 1984 Jon Speaks Award winner
★ 1985 NBA second-round draft pick (Atlanta Hawks, 41st overall pick)

April 4, 1983, was grab Whittenburg's airball from 25 feet, and stuff it through the basket. Then he started looking around to see if anyone was going to yell at him. After all, he had scored only two points in the game to that point, and no one in the building expected the ball to end up in his hands.

In fact, during the final timeout, with the game tied at 52, Valvano pulled Charles aside before he went back onto the floor and chided him for his lackadaisical effort in the most important game of his career.

"Lo, you haven't done anything all night," Valvano told him. "I wish you would wake up."

Boy, did he ever.

But after he made the shot, there was a long pause, as everyone waited to see if the officials might somehow wave off the basket. Then, pandemonium ensued.

"I never heard the buzzer," Charles said in a 1984 interview. "I couldn't hear what the guys were telling me. They were

"Here it is, more than 20 years later, and people are still talking about it. When it happened, I thought I would have my little 15 minutes of fame and that would be it."

[LORENZO CHARLES]

trying to tell me that the shot was good, the dunk was in time, that we had won."

But there was enough doubt in Charles's mind that he didn't start celebrating immediately, mainly because all he could think was that he was standing where he shouldn't have been.

"I was right up under the basket, so I had the best view of anybody on the floor," Charles says. "Had I been where Thurl was or Hakeem was, I wouldn't have jumped for fear of offensive goal-tending. That's probably why no one else made a move to the basket.

"There wasn't a whole lot of thought involved. I just went up, got my hands on the ball and put it in. I knew there wasn't much time left."

What astounds Charles, though, is that the dunk that gave the Wolfpack its 54-52 victory over the famed Phi Slamma Jamma, is still replayed over and over and over during highlights of March Madness.

"Here it is, more than 20 years later, and people are still talking about it," he says. "When it happened, I thought I would have my little 15 minutes of fame and that would be it."

But when he sees the play, there are always certain things that come to mind for

Charles, turning his demure face upside down with a broad grin. He remembers the pep rally in Reynolds Coliseum the day the team returned, and addressing the crowd wearing his long-sleeve T-shirt and his askance fishing hat.

"I remember the euphoria, the pandemonium, the all-out great college atmosphere we came back to when we returned from New Mexico," Charles said.

But what he should also remember is not only that the shot that changed the dreams of every basketball underdog, the basket that put the craziness into March Madness, was also the transforming moment of his career.

Until the Wolfpack went on its nine-game run to the ACC title and NCAA championship, Charles was a regular in the Wolfpack lineup, but he was hardly a big contributor. He left the scoring up to Whittenburg, Bailey and Sidney Lowe, the heart-and-soul seniors playing their final season of basketball.

Charles, almost negligible in the Wolfpack's first 20 games, grew up after Whittenburg suffered what was thought to be a season-ending broken foot in January. In the Wolfpack's final 13 games that year, he

"He used to try to dunk everything. I mean everything. A little child walked by, and he tried to dunk him."

[JIM VALVANO]

averaged 11.5 points and 8.5 rebounds, and scored the winning points in three of his team's nine postseason games.

By the next season, his game—and body—had completely transformed.

"He used to try to dunk everything," Valvano once said of the player who eventually evolved into an All-ACC and All-America selection. "I mean everything. A little child walked by, and he tried to dunk him."

His rippling, muscular arms earned him the nickname "Lorilla," though it was a frequent misconception that the Brooklyn, New York-born Charles was always a muscle-bound monster in the paint. He never lifted weights in high school and didn't start in college until Cozell McQueen finally shamed him into making regular trips to the weight room.

"There were times," Valvano once said of Charles, "when he couldn't run up and down the court three times without asking to be taken out."

But between his sophomore and junior seasons, spurred by the notoriety he gained from making the game-winning shot and the confidence that it gave him, Charles spent the summer lifting weights, doing 500-pound squats and dozens of pull-ups wearing a 50-pound belt.

The result was a well-defined body that had 15 more pounds of muscle than when he made his famous jam. He became a fearsome offensive player, who had a surprisingly soft touch on his mid-range jumpshots.

"He is so strong," Missouri coach Norm Stewart said of Charles following a 1984 contest. "We tried to front him and the only thing that did was give him good board position for easy putbacks. But I had promised the other players' mothers that I wouldn't put their sons on Charles."

His physical presence helped the Wolfpack win 10 of its first 12 games in 1983-84, but teams eventually learned to double- and triple-team him, taking advantage of the Wolfpack's lack of depth inside. State lost its last seven games and was not invited into the NCAA field to defend its championship.

"I think he has the greatest touch for a player his size that I have ever seen," Valvano said of his rising star following his junior season. "He's a physical-finesse player."

Charles improved so much that junior season that there were reports—unfounded, he says even today—that he might declare early for the NBA draft. But he came back as a senior and dominated, earning first-team

All-ACC honors and finishing second in the ACC Player of the Year voting to Len Bias. He helped the Wolfpack get back to the Final Eight in the NCAA Tournament, thanks to a pair of wins in a return trip to Albuquerque. But he missed out on a chance to return to the Final Four when the Wolfpack lost to St. John's in Denver in the West Region finals.

Though Charles's physique would have seemed to make him a strong prospect for the NBA, at six-foot-seven, he was just between sizes for a power forward and a small forward. He was a second-round pick (No. 41 overall) in the draft by the Atlanta Hawks.

"I was disappointed in going only in the second round," Charles says. "I honestly thought I had played to the level of what a first-round draft pick needs to play to. There are times it doesn't work out like that.

"I know size is a big deal, but I think desire is something you should measure a player on. The way the NBA goes, everybody doesn't get an equal shot. When you are not drafted in the first round, you don't get as much opportunity to be successful as a first-round pick gets. Going in the second round, opportunities for playing time were few and far between. When you are a second-round pick, you have to wait your turn, and sometimes that turn never comes."

While he played only one year in the NBA, averaging 3.4 points and 1.1 rebounds with the Hawks, he played professionally for

"His game, his size, everything that he did was perfect for college basketball."

[NATE McMILLAN]

some 13 years, in the NBA, the Continental Basketball Association and the United States Basketball Association. He played abroad in Italy, Great Britain, Spain, Uruguay, Sweden, Turkey and Argentina.

"You more or less go where the job is," Charles says.

He eventually settled down in Wake Forest, North Carolina, where he is a partner in a transportation company.

"He was a great college player," says former teammate Nate McMillan, now the coach of the Seattle SuperSonics. "His game, his size, everything that he did was perfect for college basketball. He was a monster in the paint, and he just dominated down there.

"For the pros, he was undersized, and he was just a scorer. He didn't do the other things the NBA people look for."

But on one certain night in New Mexico, Charles did exactly what was needed, even if he was in the wrong place at the right time.

NATE McMILLAN

Nate McMillan did not want to get on the plane.

The homebody who had never lived more than 100 miles away from his native Raleigh had never flown anywhere before by himself, especially not all the way across the country.

The night before, in what should have been one of the happiest times of his life, he stayed up crying with his fiancée, Michelle. When would they see each other again? If he made the final roster of the Seattle SuperSonics, the team that had just taken him in the second round of the NBA draft, it might be months. If he didn't, well, then, what would happen next?

There were so many things roiling around in McMillan's brain, he couldn't possibly think straight. All he knew was this: What the hell was he doing getting on a plane to Seattle?

The simple answer was that McMillan had a job there, as the 30th pick in the ill-fated 1986 NBA draft. It was about as far away from home as he could go and still be on the U.S. mainland. Sure, it was his favorite Western Conference team, though that may have had more to do with his dislike of the Los Angeles Lakers than any great knowledge of the Sonics. But he knew almost nothing about the town, except that it got a lot of rain.

Who would ever believe that McMillan would end up a Seattle icon, like the Space Needle, Frasier Crane and vanilla lattes?

But that summer day in the terminal of Raleigh-Durham International Airport, McMillan was balking like a stubborn plow

mule. When he found out that there was a minor mechanical problem with the plane, he took it as a sign from above that he should stay at home.

He got back in the car with his mother, his older brother Randy and his fiancé and made them take him away from the airport. But as he and Randy fussed the whole way home, age eventually won out. His mom turned the car around and the bickering group headed back to the airport. McMillan had missed his original flight, but found another that went through New York. And he couldn't find an excuse to stay off of it.

"If everybody made the same effort and played the way Nate McMillan comes to play, we could be winning this game."

[JIM VALVANO]

"I was like a kid who did not want to go to school and was trying to make his tummy ache so he wouldn't have to go," McMillan says now. "I had never been that far away from home before."

Now, after two decades of working for the SuperSonics, first as a player, then as an assistant and ultimately as the head coach, McMillan can't imagine why he was so scared. While he had his doubts that he might be a long-term player and coach in the NBA, the late Jim Valvano told his versatile point guard long before, point-blank, that he would do well on the next level.

That came as significant news to McMillan on February 9, 1985, when Valvano used McMillan as an example during a half-time chewing out of the team in the home locker room of Reynolds Coliseum. McMillan was in his first year with the Wolfpack, after transferring from Chowan Junior College in Murfreesboro, North Carolina. It was a team that had plenty of NBA potential, though some of it—namely, freshman sensation Chris Washburn—was troubled.

The Wolfpack, except for McMillan, had not played well in the first half against Southern Methodist. The point guard who grew more than four inches during his two years at junior college played as many as three positions for the Wolfpack, and this particu-

lar day, frequently displayed his leadership skills that were extremely important on this talented but immature team.

"If everybody made the same effort and played the way Nate McMillan comes to play, we could be winning this game," Valvano said. "That guy there will play 10 years in the NBA."

McMillan's eyes widened. Playing professional basketball was never his basketball dream. Even playing for N.C. State was a far-fetched goal. The only ACC team that recruited McMillan out of Raleigh's Enloe High School was Clemson, and he didn't have to grades to get into a Division I college.

But by adding height to his do-everything game, McMillan got the interest of scads of major schools: Virginia, Maryland, Clemson, Old Dominion. However, he didn't answer many phone calls after Valvano offered him a scholarship during his second year at Chowan.

"To be honest, I was a little upset that N.C. State didn't write me or contact me at all out of high school," McMillan says. "They didn't even send me a letter or send anyone to see me. I was disappointed because I just loved the team.

"And even when they did recruit me, they came in late. But when they came in, even as upset with them as I was for not recruiting me earlier, I immediately forgot all about it. I couldn't believe they were there, and I had the opportunity to play for that university."

All that could go through McMillan's mind was the first time he went to Reynolds Coliseum as a kid, one of the few trips he ever made to the fabled old arena before his playing career with the Wolfpack began.

"I actually saw Kenny Carr walk by me as a kid," McMillan remembers. "It was almost like the Coke commercial where Mean Joe Greene walks past the kid in the tunnel and throws him his jersey. I had never seen a person as big as Kenny Carr before.

"It was like seeing the Incredible Hulk for the first time."

McMillan was never a star in high school, college or in the NBA. But he was a solid contributor and an even better citizen in an era that was desperate for anyone without a felony charge.

McMillan may have grown up in a Raleigh housing project, without ever meeting his father, but he was instilled with a great sense of character and integrity by Randy, who was four years older than Nate and chiefly responsible for taking care of his younger brother while their mother worked two jobs, cleaning hotel rooms, washing dishes in restaurants, even handling housekeeping duties at an N.C. State dorm. She provided and they survived, mainly by hanging out at Lions Park, a sprawling oasis near downtown Raleigh where the two brothers could spend the bulk of their days without getting in much trouble.

McMillan came to State as part of

Valvano's most celebrated recruiting class, along with Chris Washburn, Quentin Jackson, John Thompson and Vinny Del Negro. He immediately became a leader on a team that lacked discipline.

In two years, he helped the Wolfpack make it to the Final Eight twice, losing to St. John's his first year and to Kansas his second.

"We were a game away each of my two years from reaching the Final Four," McMillan said. "If we are not playing Kansas in Kansas City, we would have probably gone to the Final Four (in 1986).

"Do you recall the officiating in the second half of that game?"

In fact, it was a hard thing to forget for a young student reporter who was covering the NCAA Tournament for the first time. The Wolfpack was leading the Jayhawks 57-52 with nine minutes to play, with ACC free-throw champion Ernie Myers on the line. Myers missed the opportunity for a three-point play, McMillan charged into Greg Dreiling on a questionable call, and Danny Manning scored 12 straight points for his team. Those things combined to set off a "Rock, Chalk, Jayhawk" rally in Kemper Arena that doomed the Wolfpack's return to the Final Four.

During his professional career, McMillan had three more opportunities to win championships. He helped the Sonics reach the Western Finals twice, and played (some, at least) for the 1996 NBA Championship against the Chicago Bulls. But McMillan had back problems in that derailed title run, and he missed the first three games of the series.

"I feel like if I was healthy, we would have beaten the Bulls."

[NATE McMILLAN]

McMillan—and most of the Emerald City—is convinced that had he not been on the bench in those three games and able to play defense against his North Carolina contemporary, Michael Jordan, that the Bulls would not have taken a three-nothing lead.

McMillan forced himself back on the court for Game 4, and helped the Sonics win the next two games. But no one ever forced the Bulls to a seven-game series as Jordan led them to six NBA titles, and the Sonics couldn't do it, either.

"I feel like if I was healthy, we would have beaten the Bulls," McMillan says, in a voice that hints of regret. "It was great to be there and be part of it. I felt like we were a very good team that year. We went against one of the best players to ever play this game. But I really do believe if I was healthy, we would have won."

The day he retired as a player, he was hired as an assistant coach. In his first season on the sidelines, McMillan's No. 10 jersey—the same number he wore at N.C. State—was retired by the Sonics, and McMillan joined Seattle legends Jack Sikma, Fred Brown and Lenny Wilkens as the franchise's only jerseys hanging from the rafters of KeyArena.

Of that honor, *Seattle Post-Intelligencer* Art Thiel wrote: "Nate McMillan might be the first athlete whose jersey was retired because he was a good teammate and a better person. That says a lot about sports. It also says a lot about this place (Seattle), rewarding someone whose celebrity profile didn't much exceed the Aurora Avenue tunnel. For a country son of the Carolinas, McMillan turned out to be as Seattle as damp floor mats."

McMillan was similarly honored by N.C. State in 2002.

On the same day that new Sonics owners fired Paul Westphal as the team's head coach, general manager (and former Virginia hero) Wally Walker offered McMillan the unexpected opportunity to become the head coach for the only NBA team he had ever played for.

"I never thought about being a head coach in the NBA," McMillan says. "It was the farthest thing from my mind. I wanted to be an assistant, I wanted to grow and gain some experience through scouting, and in 10 or 20 years, get that opportunity when I had all my notebooks full. It didn't happen that way.

"After two years, the general manager walked into my office and said, 'We want you to be the head coach.'"

McMillan was thrilled, and a little bit scared. "I needed to talk to my Mommy," he says.

Walker gave McMillan only 15 minutes to make his decision, or the club was going to offer the job to someone else. McMillan never got the chance to call his mom, his brother or his wife. He accepted the job and went to practice.

"I had to go from an assistant who was getting his notes together to becoming the head coach who was expected to address the team in 15 minutes," McMillan says. "I threw the whistle over my head and walked down the stairs and I was the head coach."

McMillan knows that Valvano would be proud of his accomplishment. The coach loved all his point guards, and was known for developing them during his 10 years as the Wolfpack's head coach, starting with Sidney Lowe and continuing with Spud Webb, McMillan and Chris Corchiani.

Now, as a coach, McMillan appreciates his playing career more than he ever did as a player. He was always content with his role as a defensive-minded point guard who passed the ball to others, which is why he ended up with 4,893 career assists, a Sonics franchise record, and 4,733 points.

So, while many people remember Valvano's 1984 recruiting class as a bust because of the embarrassing exploits of Washburn—who played little more than one season with the Wolfpack and three years in the NBA before being banned for life because of drug violations—it's interesting to note that it included two off the school's most productive NBA players: McMillan and Del Negro. Between them, they played for nearly a quarter century in the league and both had opportunities to win NBA titles.

McMillan, as the head coach of the Sonics, helped Washburn get back on his feet to some degree by giving him a favorable recommendation for a job in Texas. Washburn, the No. 3 pick of the Golden State Warriors, signed a massive contract in the summer of 1986, but squandered all of his money, mostly on drugs. By 1990, he was out of the league and begging money off former Wolfpack star Spud Webb.

It was sad situation to watch for McMillan, whose wife, Michelle, knew Washburn in high school in Hickory, North Carolina.

"She always felt Chris just grew up too fast, because of his size and because he could play basketball," McMillan says. "Because he could play, people tried to look out for him. He would always act a little more mature in high school. He was a freshman who hung out with the seniors. He was accepted because he could play basketball.

"But he always had things handed to him. He never had to work for much or anything, in a sense. That didn't happen when he got to the NBA. He had to earn the contract that was handed to him. Once you get there, you have to earn your money and earn your right to stay there and earn the right to stay an NBA athlete."

At six foot 10, Washburn was tall and athletic. He was an inside presence who could run the floor, a beautiful target for a point guard to hit with pinpoint passes, as McMillan frequently did.

"I look at him as a Shaquille O'Neal," McMillan says. He was a Shaquille who could run and jump and handle the ball. I often think about ... what he could have done in the NBA if he had stayed straight, how much money he would have made, if he had dealt with his issue or his problems. Easily, he could have been a $100 million player. It's sad because he was a helluva basketball player."

But natural talent isn't necessarily what makes a professional career, something McMillan learned in his dozen years on the Sonics roster. He always prided himself on bringing his teammates together, contributing to a long-term goal, instead of just playing for himself.

"As a coach now, I realize how important I was to a team, because I am now looking for players just like myself," McMillan says. " I can see the value of a player who is not selfish, who competes every night, who competes in the best interest of the club, a player who is versatile enough to play several different positions. I can see the value of myself now after my career and how important I was to all the teams that I played on."

He also knows the value of having strong family support, especially a big brother who can force you to get on an airplane even if you don't want to.

AP/WWP

"As a coach now, I realize how important I was to a team, because I am now looking for players just like myself."

[NATE McMILLAN]

VINNY DEL NEGRO

It's hard to say whether Vinny Del Negro had basketball career or lived a morality play. Maybe the two can be the same.

For Del Negro—who some considered the fifth wheel in Jim Valvano's heralded 1984 recruiting class that included freshmen Chris Washburn, John Thompson and Quentin Jackson and junior college transfer Nate McMillan—there was never any doubt that he was capable of having a career that would earn his jersey a hanger at N.C. State's basketball home or his sneakers a permanent place to rest at the Naismith Memorial Basketball Hall of Fame, which used to be only a few blocks down the road from where Del Negro grew up in Springfield, Massachusetts.

Del Negro just had to convince everyone else.

The first challenge was Valvano, who outrecruited Kentucky to get Del Negro to Raleigh. But for two and a half years, Del Negro spent as much time on the bench, playing behind Spud Webb, Terry Gannon and McMillan, as he did in Valvano's office, playing darts, eating popcorn and asking the coach for advice on how to improve his game enough to contribute to the Wolfpack program.

The answer—supplied not by Valvano, but by Del Negro's father, Vince Del Negro Sr.—was simply "Work harder, be better."

The elder Del Negro was not just a pushy stage dad. He had some experiences, and regrets, in basketball. A two-time junior college All-American in the 1950s, Vin Del Negro ended up playing for Adolph Rupp at Kentucky. Briefly.

After being taken out of the starting lineup a few games into the season, he lost his

VINNY DEL NEGRO

Born: August 9, 1966 (Springfield, Massachusetts)
High School: Suffield Academy, Suffield, Connecticut
Degree: B.A., Speech Communications, N.C. State, 1988
Position: Shooting guard
Number: 14 (honored)
Years with the Wolfpack: 1985-88
NCAA Tournament Appearances: 1985, '86, '87, '88
Championships: 1987 ACC Championship, 1992 Italian League Championship
Honors:
★ 1986 Tip-Off Classic Most Valuable Player Award
★ 1987 First-team All-ACC Tournament
★ 1987 Everett Case Award winner (Most Valuable Player of ACC Tournament)
★ 1987 Jon Speaks Award winner
★ 1988 First-team All-ACC selection
★ 1988 Second-team All-ACC Tournament
★ 1988 Alumni Athletic Trophy winner
★ 1988 Second-round NBA selection (Sacramento Kings, 29th overall pick)
★ 1992 Italian A League playoffs Most Valuable Player
★ Owns San Antonio Spurs franchise record with 50 consecutive free throws
★ Selected as one of the Top 25 players in San Antonio Spurs history
★ Awarded locker at the Naismith Memorial Basketball Hall of Fame in Springfield, Mass. Founder, Vinny Del Negro Endowment Fund for sexually abused and physically abused youths
★ Named one of five Most Caring Athletes by USA Weekend in 1994
★ 2001 Inductee into the New England Basketball Hall of Fame

cool with Rupp and his heart for the game. He walked away from basketball for good, without ever fulfilling the promise that enabled him to twice be the top junior college scorer in the nation.

"I was prepared, I watched and was ready to play. I let frustration creep in at times, but in the overall picture, I knew if I just continued to work and watch that my opportunity to play would come."

[VINNY DEL NEGRO]

The younger Del Negro may have had the same urge to tell Valvano what his dad screamed at Rupp during that practice when he was demoted from starter to reserve. But he didn't, thanks to his father's advice.

"When I wasn't playing, there is no question that frustration set in," Del Negro says. "My father told me, 'Vinny, if you are good enough, the coach is going to play you.'"

Most teenagers don't want to hear that. They are more willing to listen to friends or family who say, "You're better than the other guy. Why aren't you playing?" Or "That coach doesn't like you. You should get out of there."

In fact, one of Valvano's legacies is of players who came for a short period of time, then headed elsewhere. At least six of Del Negro's would-be teammates transferred elsewhere just in his first two seasons: Russell Pierre, Walker Lambiotte, Andy Kennedy, Kenny Drummond, Sean Green and John Thompson.

But that never really became an option for Del Negro. He had chosen his path, with the help of his close-knit Italian family, and he vowed to continue following it.

"If you have good guidance and you sit down and look at those things objectively, the coach wants to win," Del Negro says now, with the benefit of two good decades of life experiences. "My dad told me this: the coach is going to put the best players on the court that he feels will give the team the best opportunity to win. I sat back and said, 'Hey, if I am really as good as I think I am, then I am going to get that opportunity.'

"That's what happened for me. I was prepared, I watched and was ready to play. I let frustration creep in at times, but in the overall picture, I knew if I just continued to work and watch that my opportunity to play would come. I knew I could handle it once it did appear. I knew of my father's experiences in basketball. We had talked about them. I did the same thing with Coach Valvano."

As a kid, Del Negro was both a gym rat and Gym rat. He had a three-pickup-game-a-day habit around the mid-sized city, where in 1893 Springfield College physical education professor James Naismith nailed up a couple of peach baskets at the school's volleyball court and basketball was born. The rest of the time, Del Negro hauled ice around his father's package store and (later) sports bar, called, appropriately enough, Vin's Gym.

He left home at age 14, to become a full-time basketball player and student at Suffield Academy in Connecticut, about 30 minutes from home, but practically a universe away for a working class kid from Springfield. Still, Del Negro flourished, helping his new school win two state prep school championships, including an undefeated senior season. His prep career was honored in 2001 when he was in the inaugural class of the New England Basketball Hall of Fame.

Kentucky came calling, with coach Joe B. Hall and assistant Leonard Hamilton showing up in coats and ties, and they made a strong pitch for the kid whose favorite college player was Kyle Macy. Valvano came in with a different air, not to mention a shared Italian heritage and an audio tape that was both improbable and prophetic. Valvano and assistant Tom Abatemarco, wearing warmup suits, met Del Negro and his family at Suffield coach Dennis Kinne's house, and played the tape, which had Wolfpack radio man Garry Dornburg pretending to announce Del Negro as the hero of a future ACC Tournament game.

By the time the night was over, Del Negro was high-fiving and celebrating with Valvano and Abatemarco for the fantastic finish. Then Del Negro took the coaches to a restaurant where his cousin was a chef.

"The great thing about recruiting Italian kids is that you don't have to feed them, they feed you," Valvano once told Don Markus of the *Baltimore Sun*.

Kentucky never had a chance.

But for the first two and a half years of Del Negro's college experience, there was little reason to throw a celebration feast. He played in just 36 of the Wolfpack's 67 games as a freshman and sophomore, scoring a grand total of 68 points. Not until the early part of the season did Del Negro earn his starting spot in the lineup, and that was never assured until late January, when point guard Kenny Drummond abruptly left the program, leaving the Wolfpack with a back-court of Del Negro and Jackson.

The Wolfpack opened the 1986-87 season by playing David Robinson and Navy in the Tip-Off Classic in Springfield. In typical, Valvano-inspired storybook fashion, Del Negro was one of the stars of the upset, leading his team to an 86-84 victory over his future NBA teammate by scoring 19 points in just 17 minutes of action.

But he went back to the bench until a January game against Georgia Tech, and was rewarded with a permanent position in the starting lineup. The six-foot-five combination guard ended up starting the final 20 games of his junior season, and by the time the ACC Tournament rolled around he was one of the team's most important links, with his outside-shooting, ball-handling, clutch free-throw shooting and rebounding abilities.

His performance in the ACC Tournament, following the Wolfpack's disappointing 6-8 regular-season finish, was a basketball daydreamer's wish come true. He had 15 points and 12 rebounds in the Wolfpack's overtime victory against Duke in the first round, 12 points and five rebounds in the double-overtime victory over Wake Forest in the semifinals and scored the winning two free throws with 14 seconds remaining in the championship game against North Carolina.

An 89 percent free-throw shooter for his junior year, Del Negro was perfect at the line in the final five minutes of the tournament, hitting all 10 of his attempts down the stretch.

All of a sudden, celebrating that fake championship with Valvano and Abatemarco three years earlier didn't seem so ridiculous. Del Negro became the hero of the Wolfpack's 10th ACC Championship team and won the Everett Case Award as the tournament's Most Valuable Player.

Del Negro came back the following year and became a first-team All-ACC selection, a well-developed all-around player who was eventually picked early in the second round of the NBA draft by the Sacramento Kings.

Del Negro's eventual success always made Valvano burst with pride. The coach had a similar playing career at Rutgers, where he arrived as a walk-on and ended up being a surprise star in the school's run to the semifinals of the 1967 National Invitation Tournament.

"Vinny didn't always play that much, but he waited, gained maturity, gained strength, improved his game and then, when the opportunity came, he was ready for it," Valvano once told Charles Chandler of the *Durham Herald*. "I respect guys like that in a special way because of their ability to believe

> # "I think Vinny's career, to be perfectly honest with you, is the way a college career is supposed to be."
>
> [JIM VALVANO]

in themselves, their coaches, the program and winning. They make themselves better without compromising.

"I think Vinny's career, to be perfectly honest with you, is the way a college career is supposed to be. If I had my druthers, they'd all be that way. It's the way I remember it."

Del Negro's reward for his patience and persistence resulted in a long professional career, that had some similar twists and turns. He spent two years in Sacramento playing for the Kings, but didn't particularly like the direction the team was headed, so he turned down a contract extension in favor of a three-year guaranteed contract with Benetton Treviso of the Italian A League. Del Negro was no stranger to the team's general manager, Beppe DeStefano, who had scouted the player just after his career with the Wolfpack ended.

Jumping to play in Europe was not all that uncommon at the time. Duke's Danny Ferry had done it, as had Brian Shaw and Michael Cooper. But Del Negro, despite

> "I knew if I kept working hard, watching other players, getting stronger, that I would get the opportunity. No one was going to stop me."
>
> [VINNY DEL NEGRO]

Sacramento's intentions to re-sign him, followed his heart and went overseas. He was only a generation removed from Italian immigrants, which enabled him to get an Italian passport.

He ended up becoming a cult hero in his team's small town, a few miles outside Venice. He and his wife, Lynn, who he met as a junior at N.C. State, were highly visible patrons of the town's cafes and bistros. He became an even bigger celebrity when, in his second year there, he led Benetton Treviso to the Italian A League Championship, a franchise first, and was named the Most Valuable Player of the A League Tournament.

That opened the door for the rest of his professional career. The San Antonio Spurs signed Del Negro after his second year in Italy, and he spent six years playing with David Robinson and Company. He was a valuable member of a team that at the time was one of the best in the NBA. He was named one of the top 25 players in Spurs history during the franchise's celebration of its silver anniversary and he still owns the team record with 50 consecutive free throws. After his contract with the Spurs ended, Del Negro spent four more years in the league, with stops in Milwaukee, Golden State and Phoenix before retiring in 2001, ending a 14-year professional career that early doubters would have thought impossible.

Del Negro never doubted himself for a minute.

"It's funny, because people say that all the time," Del Negro says. "Everybody wants to talk about not playing my first couple of years at N.C. State, and how disappointing it must have been. But I knew what abilities I had. I knew if I continued to develop and get stronger and play in the summer league and watch what guys like Nate McMillan and Spud Webb did, that I could succeed.

"I knew if I kept working hard, watching other players, getting stronger, that I would get the opportunity. No one was going to stop me."

Del Negro made sure to inspire others on the way. He and his wife spent hours, in season and out of season, doing charity work, and in 1994 he was one of five people named by *USA Weekend* as Most Caring Athlete, thanks to his work with Brightside for Families and Children in West Springfield, Massachusetts, and his long-running basketball camp in Sacramento. He was recognized by the Texas legislature in 1997 for his work in raising money for the San Antonio school district through All-Star Connection.

Now, after settling down with his wife in the Phoenix area, Del Negro is embarking on his post-playing career, which includes time as a television analyst, developing three business ventures and occasional weekends playing on the Celebrity Players Tour, a golf tour for former athletes and other celebrities.

In 2001, he was given a locker in a portion of the old Naismith Memorial Basketball Hall of Fame that honors Springfield locals who have done well in basketball and his No. 14 jersey was honored by N.C. State. It now hangs in the rafters of the RBC Center with most of the other greats of Wolfpack basketball.

And, if you ask him today as he enjoys life after a long basketball career, Del Negro will tell you it was all worth the wait.

CHUCKY BROWN

The thing Chris Corchiani remembers about Chucky Brown is that he was one of the best teammates he ever had. Not necessarily the best player, mind you, but the best kind of guy to have in the locker room and on the court. Brown even won N.C. State's Jon Speaks Best Teammate Award in 1989.

Which is a good thing, because during his 13-year NBA career, Brown was a teammate of just about everybody who played professional basketball in the 1990s, from his childhood idol James Worthy with the Los Angeles Lakers to Eldridge Recasner, who became Brown's best friend as they played on four different franchises in two different leagues.

"There's somebody on every team I have played with," Brown said near the end of his career.

By the time he finally finished playing in 2002, Brown he had played for 12 different NBA franchises in 13 years, which ties him with former Maryland player Tony Massenburg for the most teams in a career. And that doesn't include his stints in Italy and the Continental Basketball Association.

Brown may have been a journeyman most of his career, but in 1995, when he made the jump from the CBA's franchise in Yakima, Washington, to the Houston Rockets, he enabled himself to win something only two other former N.C. State players have ever done: win an NBA Championship ring.

Only former All-American John Richter, who was a member of the 1960 champion Boston Celtics, and seven-foot-five center Chuck Nevitt, who won a pair of rings

CHUCKY BROWN

Born: February 28, 1968 (New York, New York)
High School: North Brunswick High School, Leland, North Carolina
Degree: B.A., Sociology, N.C. State, 2005
Position: Forward
Number: 52
Years with the Wolfpack: 1985-89
NCAA Tournament Appearances: 1986, '87, '88, '89
Championships: 1987 ACC championship; 1995 NBA championship (Houston Rockets), 1995 CBA Championship (Yakima Sun Kings)
Honors:
★ Third highest career field goal percentage at 55.7 percent
★ 1987 Second-team All-ACC Tournament
★ 1989 First-team All-ACC selection
★ 1989 Jon Speaks Award
★ Second-round NBA selection (Cleveland Cavaliers, 43rd pick overall)
★ Shares NBA record for most teams played for in a career with 12

with the Los Angeles Lakers and Chicago Bulls, can claim the same distinction.

Brown was burning up the CBA with a 21.6 scoring average after 31 games when the defending NBA champion Houston Rockets came calling for some inside help, a call Brown's agent got so many times during Brown's career. The Rockets, however, were the best team Brown ever played for. He started out with two 10-day contracts, but was eventually signed for the rest of the season, filling in for the Rockets' loss of Otis Thorpe, Vernon Maxwell, Carl Herrera and Robert Horry and averaging 6.2 points and 4.7 rebounds for the champions.

"I ended up being a key player, and I got to play for my ring."

[CHUCKY BROWN]

Charles Barkley, then with the Phoenix Suns, famously said during the Western Conference finals "Who is Chucky Brown? I don't even know him," when Brown was assigned to defend Barkley. It didn't take long for Barkley—who later apologized privately to Brown for his public slight—to find out, as Brown played well enough during his 61 games with the Rockets that year to earn a two-year contract with the club.

"I ended up being a key player, and I got to play for my ring," said Brown, who was used as the top reserve coming off the bench.

In fact, Brown won two championships that year, since Yakima went on to win the CBA crown. Brown, who played almost the entire season with the Sun Kings, got a ring for that title, too, becoming only the second player in history to win titles with two teams the same season.

Brown was never a superstar, never a guy to build a team around, either in college or in professional basketball. At six feet, eight inches, he was at an in-between size for small forward and power forward. But he was productive, a standup guy in a sometimes shady profession who was always willing to pitch in and do whatever was needed. His happy-go-lucky personality made him a popular guy in the locker room, as did his attitude on the floor, where he understood the value of being nothing more than a team player.

"If you look at Liberace, he was the only one on stage playing the piano," Brown once told Sherrod Blakely of the Raleigh *News & Observer*. "But he didn't bring the piano up there by himself. He didn't set up all the lights and other stuff around the piano by himself. There were others. That's how I see my role as being. Someone who does a lot of the dirty work, doesn't get much credit, but someone that's important to the team."

Brown learned to play basketball on the playgrounds of Harlem, where his family lived until he was 15 years old. He played football and baseball in school, but never organized basketball. But that was in the early 1980s, when the Big Apple was at its dirtiest and deadliest. Brown's father, Clarence, saw how bad the city had become from his driver's seat in a New York City transit bus, where he sat for 27 years. He wanted to get his son and daughter, Toni, out.

So they left the family matriarch, Minnie, who was a couple of years away from retirement from the phone company, behind and moved back to Clarence's hometown, Navassa, North Carolina, a small coastal community on the other side of the Cape Fear River from Wilmington. Chucky played on his first school team as a sophomore at Leland's New Brunswick High School, twice earning All-State honors, making the rounds to the various all-star camps and team camps and playing on a U.S. Junior team that traveled to West Germany in the summer of 1985.

He knew early on that he wanted to play for Jim Valvano, after the Wolfpack coach came to his parents' house one evening and started moving all the furniture around to set up some living room basketball plays.

"My parents thought he was crazy," Brown says. "I knew he was, and I wanted to play for him."

Brown started five games early in his freshman year, while teammate Charles Shackleford sat out for academic reasons. But he played only sparingly the rest of the season, averaging just 3.1 points a game. It was the source of frustration that he didn't get the playing time he thought he deserved.

"There were many times I was frustrated because of not getting to play, but my dad would always tell me that my time would come, just keep working hard," Brown says. "He just kept saying that. I just wanted to know when that time was going to come. I only had four years.

"But then I watched a guy like Vinny Del Negro, who didn't play much for two and a half years and then he got his chance to play, too."

Del Negro was a junior when he finally got his big chance in 1987; Brown was a sophomore that year, and still played only sparingly. But the two were terrific in the Wolfpack's run to the ACC Championship, leading the Pack in an overtime win over Duke, a double-overtime win over Wake Forest and a one-point victory over North Carolina, which had not lost to an ACC opponent all season until the title game.

Del Negro won the MVP of that tournament, but Brown was also an unlikely hero, scoring a career-high 18 points and grabbing 11 rebounds against the Tar Heels in the title game.

"That was one of the most gratifying things in my career," Brown says.

As a sophomore, Brown doubled his scoring and rebounding average from his freshman year. Then he did it again as a junior. By the time he was a senior, he was being recognized for his unselfish play and productivity, as the Wolfpack was a surprising winner of the ACC regular-season race. Brown, who led the ACC in rebounding at 8.8 boards a game in 1989, joined teammate Rodney Monroe as a first-team All-ACC selection.

After finishing his career as one of the top 20 scorers in school history and recording the third best field goal shooting percentage ever at State, Brown was a second-round selection in the 1989 NBA draft by the Cleveland Cavaliers, the 43rd pick overall. Just getting to that point, something not even Brown's parents really thought was possible, was one of Brown's biggest achievements.

"I had people walking around here telling me I wouldn't make it," Brown says. "So it was satisfying not only to make it, but to play in the league for 13 years and to win a ring. Some of the greatest players in history don't have a ring."

Brown's hard work was always recognized, by coaches like Paul Silas and general managers who needed a strong plug-in at the end of the season. Brown even had the support of an ardent, spell-casting fan club,

> # "I had people walking around here telling me I wouldn't make it. So it was satisfying not only to make it, but to play in the league for 13 years and to win a ring. Some of the greatest players in history don't have a ring."
>
> [CHUCKY BROWN]

three dozen members of which once picketed outside the Summit in Houston when Brown was traded, along with Sam Cassell and Robert Horry, from the Rockets to the Suns for Brown's uninformed rival, Barkley.

He saw a little of everything—not to mention every corner of the North American continent—during his career, which ranged from a one-game stint (in which he made the only shot he attempted) in Dallas in 1994 to 82 consecutive starts for Houston in 1996. But when he decided to finally settle down, he wanted to be back near N.C. State. So he bought a home in Cary, where he lives with his wife and two daughters.

"He always worked on his game, and worked to get better," says Del Negro, who was Brown's teammate for three years at N.C. State and one year at Golden State. "He worked hard, understood his role and went out and did his job everyday. I think that is why he played for so many years. Teams knew he would make the effort and prepare properly.

"I think guys who have the opportunity to be successful in the NBA are guys who understand how they can make their team better and what they do really well to incorporate that into the team, whether it is being a great shooter, a great rebounder, a great passer, great defender, great leader. If you can incorporate one or two or three of those things into a team that needs a certain element, then your success and longevity is assured."

For Brown, adding those little components to every team allowed him to play for more years and contribute to more teams than he ever thought possible.

LES
ROBINSON

Les Robinson was pissed.

Here he was, a 17-year-old freshman, invited to go to the movies with the senior captain of the basketball team, a big night out on the town for a kid from St. Albans, West Virginia. But before they went to the theater, Stan Niewierowski parked his car in front of a bar on Hillsborough Street.

"Even better," Robinson thought, "we're going to get some beer."

But as Robinson reached for the door handle to get out, Niewierowski shot him a nasty look and said, "Wait here."

Little did Robinson know that Niewierowski was going inside to place a bet. Little did he know there were State Bureau of Investigations officers watching everything that was happening. Little did he know that going on all around him were the events that would kill the Dixie Classic and break Everett Case's heart.

All Robinson wanted was a glass of beer and a trip to the movies.

Niewierowski was one of four Wolfpack teammates who admitted participation in the point-shaving scandal that rocked college basketball in the early 1960s, leaving a major scar on the Wolfpack program, a disgrace Case never fully overcame. The Dixie Classic was cancelled and basketball was de-emphasized at both N.C. State and North Carolina.

As it turned out, it was Robinson's first brush with many troubled times he would face at N.C. State, the school and program he loved dearly. Even though he had to make some personal and professional sacrifices to help fix those problems—he never got to finish his playing career, he lost his job when

LES ROBINSON

Born: September 23, 1942 (St. Albans, West Virginia)
High School: St. Albans High School, St. Albans, West Virginia
Degrees: B.S. Recreation and Physical Education, NC State, 1965; Masters, Physical Education and Guidance Counseling, Western Carolina, 1968.
Position: Guard, assistant coach, head coach, athletics director
Number: 42
Years with the Wolfpack: 1962-64 (player), 1965-66 (assistant coach), 1991-96 (head coach), 1996-2000 (athletics director).
Record: 78-98 in six years at N.C. State; 291-330 overall in 22 years
NCAA Tournament Appearances: 1991
Honors:
★ N.C. State freshman basketball coach 1964, '65
★ Winningest coach in school history at The Citadel, East Tennessee State University
★ Southern Conference Coach of the Year (1979, '90)
★ NCAA Tournament Selection Committee member (1999-2004)
★ Athletics director at East Tennessee State, N.C. State and The Citadel

Press Maravich abruptly left the school for LSU and he was forced to resign from his dream job as the Wolfpack's head basketball coach—it never diminished Robinson's love of what Case had built when he arrived in 1946.

As a player, Robinson barely got off the bench in his two years as a varsity letterwinner. In his own self-deprecating manner, Robinson loves to tell the story about the 1963 ACC Tournament, when the heavily favored Wolfpack was down by 12 points to Clemson—Clemson, of all teams—in the second half. Robinson knew Case had

"I made it clear that there was no place in America that I would rather coach. I even had some other offers—South Carolina called me after my first year at State— but I only wanted to coach here."

[LES ROBINSON]

thrown in the towel when the coach put Robinson into the game. But Robinson's hustle helped the Wolfpack come back to tie the game in the waning minutes.

During a timeout, Case apparently caught on that Robinson was still in the game.

"What's he doing in there?" Case bellowed at assistant Press Maravich. "We can win this thing."

And the Pack did, 79-78, the last of Case's 15 ACC tournament victories.

As a coach, Robinson arrived at his alma mater during the aftermath of the Jim Valvano era, when there was great distrust between the school's athletics and academics departments. He not only had to handle the after-effects of the one-year probation that the school served in Valvano's last year, he had to recruit under extremely tight academic restrictions that were far tougher than any other schools in the ACC.

Besides the scholarship reductions and off-campus recruiting limitations that were part of the NCAA sanction, the school required all freshmen basketball players to have at least a 1.8 grade point average after their first year, a restriction above NCAA limits that no other school had to follow.

Robinson lost one of his first recruits, Chuck Kornegay, because of a clerical problem regarding that steadfast rule, and from that point on, opposing coaches used the restrictions against Robinson and his staff on the recruiting trail.

"We were just killed in recruiting," Robinson says.

He lost players like Donald Williams and Jerry Stackhouse, who both indicated that they were coming to N.C. State, to North Carolina.

It didn't help that from 1991-93, Duke and North Carolina won three consecutive NCAA titles, while the Wolfpack was trying to overcome a lead weight in recruiting.

Robinson still maintains, however, that he never wanted to coach anywhere else.

"I made it clear," Robinson says, "that there was no place in America that I would rather coach. I even had some other offers— South Carolina called me after my first year at State—but I only wanted to coach here."

Robinson immediately reinstituted some of the traditions Case brought with him from Indiana, like turning down the lights for pregame introductions. He

"I always hoped that I would be someone who helped bring the people back together."

[LES ROBINSON]

replaced the rubbery Tartan playing surface at Reynolds Coliseum with the wooden floor that had been mothballed two decades before. He brought up memories of Case every chance he got.

But, working under restrictions imposed by the athletics department, he couldn't win in the recruiting wars and was rarely successful on the court, though he is awfully proud of his five wins over North Carolina, including a season sweep in 1991-92.

After taking the Wolfpack to a 20-11 record and its only NCAA Tournament appearance under him in 1991, Robinson had five consecutive losing seasons. Because of the Wolfpack's frequent finishes in the bottom part of the standings, fans around the conference began to call the ACC Tournament play-in game the "Les Robinson Invitational," something that made even Robinson laugh.

So, should Robinson, who played and coached during the two least successful decades in Wolfpack basketball history, be considered a legend of the program?

Absolutely.

He was the perfect healer during two eras of distress and unrest at N.C. State, exactly what you might expect of a guy who was once the volunteer fire chief of Cedar Key, Florida. He was always willing to make per-

sonal and professional sacrifices to extinguish the flames of discontent with his affable nature.

"I always hoped that I would be someone who helped bring the people back together," Robinson says.

Robinson spent one year as a full-time assistant under Maravich, but turned to the high school ranks when Maravich went to LSU. He went 41-9 in two years, then took an assistant's position at Western Carolina for one season before taking a similar post at the Citadel. He was promoted to head coach at the Charleston, South Carolina, military school in 1975, the same position Norm Sloan once had.

Robinson stayed at that job for 11 years, winning more games than any coach in school history. In 1979, he guided the Bulldogs to 20 wins and was named the Southern Conference coach of the year.

In 1985, Robinson was hired to take over an East Tennessee State program that was coming off probation. He built a Top-25 program there, winning two more Southern Conference Coach of the Year awards.

In December 1989, Robinson brought his Buccaneers to Reynolds Coliseum for a preholiday nonconference game. Valvano had survived the initial investigations into his program with a relatively light probation, but that season brought new allegations about point-shaving and drug use by some of his players. On that very day, the Wolfpack players had been devastated to learn that center Avie Lester would not be eligible to play his entire senior season because of an administrative miscommunication.

Before the game began, the embattled Valvano met Robinson at half court.

"He said precisely, and I will swear this on the Bible, 'This might be a damned good place for you to coach, because my ass is out of here at the end of the season,'" Robinson says.

The Buccaneers, led by an electric point guard named Keith "Mister" Jennings, beat the Wolfpack, 92-82, and Wolfpack fans had an automatic favorite to be Valvano's replacement when the inevitable finally happened.

He was hired in the spring of 1990 to take over the reins Case once held, making a fast effort to re-recruit the players who were supposed to return. He went for a jog with Chris Corchiani, who had vowed to transfer if Valvano was forced out. He went to Maryland to visit with Rodney Monroe. He spent time with Tom Gugliotta, Bryant Feggins and Kevin Thompson.

Robinson counts that recruiting effort among his first successes. But when he settled down in the job, he began to realize the dire nature of the situation he was inheriting, with the massive schism between the school's academics and athletics.

"The faculty hated men's basketball," Robinson says. "That's not overstating it in the least. The general consensus was, they would have been happy to do away with college basketball and go to Division III."

Robinson eventually discovered that there were some reasons for that hatred. Valvano was the highest paid coach in college basketball. He had graduated only eight of the 40 players he recruited during his 10 years at the school. He was responsible for recruiting Chris Washburn, the six-foot-10 All-America high school player who, it was later learned in court documents, scored only 470 on the SAT. In all, Valvano recruited and the school admitted eight players who scored less than 600 on the SAT.

Still, foremost in the minds of the academics, in 1985, a Duke professor named Victor Strandberg stood up in front of the national convention of Phi Beta Kappa and denounced N.C. State's application for admission into the prestigious organization because the graduation rate of the basketball program was "absolutely reprehensible."

"I did a little checking into that," Robinson says. "Then I started thinking, and I thought if I was an English professor on this campus and any other unit on campus kept me from having the same prestige as North Carolina, Duke and Davidson, I'd be mad, too.

"But without taking sides, I still don't understand what basketball's graduation rates have to do with the Phi Beta Kappa chapter."

Robinson helped, in some small way, to fix that problem, too. In 1994, the school resubmitted its application and was granted a chapter, joining UNC, Duke, Davidson, UNC-Greensboro and Wake Forest among the state schools in the selective organization.

Robinson often joked that his epitaph would read: "Couldn't coach a lick, but he got 'em in Phi Beta Kappa."

He also recruited one of the chapter's first members, six-foot-10 center Todd Fuller, who was an academic All-American in 1995 and '96. Robinson remembers that, after all the hubbub, when Fuller graduated in 1996, having made only one B his entire college career, that there was no one around to acknowledge the feat.

"I got my wife (Barbara) to take a picture of the two of us," Robinson says, "but that was it."

In March 1996, following his fifth consecutive losing season, Robinson resigned as basketball coach. He had been offered a two-year contract extension, but he chose not to accept it because he had gotten angry mail from frustrated Wolfpack supporters who were again eager for more success on the court. One fan even sent a picture of two wolves in a death struggle.

"That had as much as anything to do with me deciding to step down," Robinson says. "I didn't want the wolves fighting with each other. Plus, I didn't like where the game was going, especially in recruiting. I didn't want to walk back out there and deal with the people you had to deal with in recruiting."

Robinson accepted an associate athletics director position at the school, but only four months later he was named as Todd Turner's replacement as athletics director, a position he had held for four years at East Tennessee State. He remained a link to the school's past, yet took the athletics depart-ment into the future by overseeing the completion of the long-awaited $158 million Entertainment and Sports Arena.

A favorite memory of Robinson's sense of humor came in 1999, as the men's basketball team was preparing for one of its many last games in Reynolds Coliseum. Robinson took a group of reporters through the halls and basement of Reynolds, remembering the old coliseum's heyday. We ended up in his office, and Robinson showed off various plaques and citations on the wall. He eventually stopped in front of a framed certificate that read "Distinguished West Virginian."

"They gave me that for marrying outside my immediate family," Robinson says.

One of his last acts as athletics director was conducting a protracted search for a football coach after the school fired Mike O'Cain. He went after, and procured, another N.C. State graduate to fill the job, Chuck Amato, who had been an assistant coach to Bobby Bowden for 18 years at Florida State.

With the opening of the ESA (now the RBC Center) and the hiring of Amato, after disappointing performances for nearly a decade in basketball and football, N.C. State signaled that it was ready to begin competing on the same level as the rest of the ACC again.

And Robinson, who dearly loves his alma mater, should get credit for helping heal some of the wounds he inherited when he replaced Valvano in 1990.

"A lot of people don't appreciate the job that Les did," says former Wolfpack star Vann Williford. "He had restrictions that

AP/WWP

nobody else had and most people don't know about. Les never for a minute would say it was not a level playing field.

"I think he did an admirable job with it. We couldn't recruit the way everybody else did, but he would never sit up and say: 'This is why.'"

Former star Chris Corchiani, who played his senior season under Robinson and maintained close contact with his former coach, agreed that Robinson had an important tenure at N.C. State, even if there were more losses than wins.

"I thought Les Robinson had a great impact on Wolfpack basketball," Corchiani says. "He was a bridge from the troubled times when he came in to the success that the program is having now. He didn't have as much success as he would have liked, or as much success that the Wolfpack faithful would have liked him to have, but he put the train back on the track."

"I thought Les Robinson had a great impact on Wolfpack basketball."

[CHRIS CORCHIANI]

FIRE & ICE

From one of the first times they played together as N.C. State teammates, it became hard to separate Chris Corchiani and Rodney Monroe, the Wolfpack's famed "Fire & Ice" guard combination.

Granted, in that one particular pickup game at Carmichael Gym, the difficulty was in prying the two flailing guards apart, so intent were they on beating each other's brains out.

It was the fall of their freshman year, and both Corchiani and Monroe had arrived as well-decorated high school point guards. Oh, Corchiani, the McDonald's All-American who was twice named Florida's "Mr. Basketball" in his career at Miami Lakes High School, had heard that Monroe wanted to play the shooting guard position in college, but he also knew from their meetings at the summer basketball camps that Monroe had played the point for four years at St. Maria Goretti High School in Baltimore, Maryland.

He had also heard from some older, trouble-making teammates that Monroe might want to play the point, and Corchiani was out to make sure nobody messed with his turf. So at one point in the endless afternoon, Monroe called a foul on Corchiani. First, they got in each other's faces. Then they started swinging. Then Chucky Brown, who stepped in as a peacemaker, got a fat lip.

Two more times, Corchiani and Monroe let their tempers take over and needed to be separated by their new teammates. The next day they were sore and bruised. Corchiani's jaw hurt.

"Nobody was going to back down," Monroe says, smiling at the memory. "I think

CHRIS CORCHIANI

Born: March 28, 1968 (Coral Gables, Florida)
High School: Miami Hialeah Lakes High School, Hialeah, Florida
Degree: B.A., Communications, N.C. State, 1993
Position: Point guard
Number: 13 (honored)
Years with the Wolfpack: 1987-91
NCAA Tournament Appearances: 1988, '89, '91
Honors:
★ First player in NCAA history to reach 1,000 assists; finished career with 1,038
★ Owns school record with 4,097 minutes played
★ Holds school record with 328 career steals
★ Led ACC in 1989 at 8.6 assists per game, '91 at 9.6 assists per game
★ Led ACC in 1988 with 1.9 steals per game, in '89 with 2.6 steals per game, in '90 with 3.2 steals per game
★ 1989, '91 Second-team All-ACC selection
★ 1991 Second-team All-ACC Tournament
★ 1991 Jon Speaks Award co-winner
★ 1991 Alumni Athletic Trophy co-winner
★ 1991 H.C. Kennett Award winner
★ 1987 McDonald's All-American

RODNEY MONROE

Born: April 16, 1968 (Hagerstown, Maryland)
High School: Saint Maria Goretti High School, Hagerstown, Maryland
Position: Shooting guard
Number: 21 (honored)
Years with the Wolfpack: 1987-91
NCAA Tournament Appearances: 1988, '89, '91
Honors:
★ N.C. State's all-time leading scorer with 2,551 career points
★ Owns school record with 322 career 3-pointers
★ Led ACC in scoring in 1991 at 27.0 points per game
★ Led ACC in free throw percentage in 1991 at 88.5 percent
★ 1987 McDonald's All-American
★ 1988 Second-team All-ACC Tournament
★ 1989, '91 First-team All-ACC selection

that is when our relationship really got started, after those rough-and-tumble incidents."

And after a trip to talk to head coach Jim Valvano, who heard about the scuffles from other players on the team. The coach, who envisioned four years of having the two guards run his transition offense, was hardly thrilled that they were at each other's throats from the first tip.

"He told us, in his own way, that we needed to work together," Corchiani remembers. "He told us we were the backcourt of the future, and we better start behaving that way."

That was really the beginning of a friendship that eventually ended with Corchiani, the emotional "Fire" part of the combination, becoming the NCAA's all-time assists leader and Monroe, the stone-faced shooter known as "Ice," breaking David Thompson's school scoring record.

Could they have done the same thing had they not played their entire college careers together? That's the perfect chicken-and-egg question for the two guards. Would Monroe have scored so many points (2,551, third most in ACC history) had Corchiani not been there to throw him the ball? Would Corchiani have had so many assists (1,038, now the second most in NCAA history behind Duke's Bobby Hurley) if Monroe hadn't been there to hit so many baskets?

"I don't know if you can answer that question," Monroe says, some 15 years after their playing days together have ended. "We both could have had good careers if we had gone to other schools and played with different people. Chris is a true point guard; all he needed was someone to pass the ball to. He could have played with another shooting guard and had a very successful career. I could have played with another point guard and been pretty good.

"Would we have been as good as we were together? It's hard to say, but I don't think so."

But Corchiani believes their special bond on the court may have been a detriment to both of them when it came to assessing their value in the NBA, where both desperately wanted to have success.

"We benefited from our play together in college, but I think we hurt one another for the next level," Corchiani says. "The scouts told me I was too dependent on Rodney, and that I never developed into a scorer or a shooter, and that he was too dependent on me to handle the ball."

But during their magical careers, which included three trips to the NCAA

"Would we have been as good as we were together? It's hard to say, but I don't think so."

[RODNEY MONROE]

"He was that way on and off the court," Corchiani says. "Whether he was walking to class or at a nighclub or in the middle of an overtime, he was always very, very reserved. Nothing ever got to him."

At least not outwardly. Monroe could get riled, but he mainly used it as motivation.

Chucky Brown remembers the night before the Wolfpack was supposed to play Iowa in the second round of the 1989 NCAA Tournament. He and Monroe were riding in an elevator at the team hotel in Providence, Rhode Island, with, of all people, Iowa stars B.J. Armstrong and Roy Marble.

The four opponents knew exactly who the others were, but Marble and Armstrong began a derogatory conversation between themselves for the benefit of Brown and Monroe. They were talking about how they had been in such big games, like their win that year at North Carolina, and how N.C. State had not. They talked freely about how they were going to win the game the next day.

"We were looking at each other like, 'Damn, we just came in first place in the ACC,'" Brown says. "But we didn't want to start nothing."

The Wolfpack teammates kept their silence throughout the elevator ride, but when they got off and the doors closed, Monroe turned to Brown and said: "Let's go kick their mother******* ass."

And you know what? Monroe did, almost singlehandedly. He scored 40 points in the double-overtime victory, including game-tying baskets in both regulation and in the first overtime. The second shot was

Tournament, the two were the inseparable combination of "Fire & Ice," a promotional name given to them by N.C. State sports information director Mark Bockelman.

"The name was perfect, because it fit our personalities so well," Monroe says.

Even in his high school days, Monroe was hard to rile. He never argued with officials' calls. He never got in anyone's face. Only once did he ever get into a fight with a teammate, and that was probably more Corchiani's fault.

"I loved doing that kind of thing at home, getting right in somebody's face, because it always got the crowd into it.

[CHRIS CORCHIANI]

over a swarming double-team by Armstrong and Marble.

At one point in the game, Marble told Brown, "He ain't going to keep shooting that good."

Brown responded: "He will if you keep leaving him open."

Monroe, who had already made an improbable tip-in with two seconds remaining in the regular-season finale against Wake Forest to send the game into a record four overtimes, made a career out of making clutch plays. As a senior, he scored 47 points against Georgia Tech and was named the ACC's Player of the Year.

Wolfpack fans will always remember Corchiani's hard-scrabble toughness. He never made first-team All-ACC, but few guards ever had more control of the pace of games than Corchiani did.

Nor did they generate as much emotion. Corchiani remembers many games when he was smacked, slapped and kicked you know where. Sometimes he goaded opponents into doing those very things.

"I didn't really mind," Corchiani says. "They would get frustrated with the way I played and do something like that. When that happened, I knew I had won. That was part of my game.

"I loved doing that kind of thing at home, getting right in somebody's face, because it always got the crowd into it."

Corchiani was always willing to do whatever Valvano asked, whether it was defending Georgia Tech center Tom Hammonds in a trademark junk defense or cooling his head after Valvano's departure finally came about.

Loyal to his head coach, Corchiani vowed that if Valvano left, he was going too. "I don't care if John Wooden is the next head coach, I am not staying," he said at the time. Monroe countered by considering his professional basketball options.

Valvano, who had already accepted a $600,000 buy-out from the school, invited Corchiani to lunch one afternoon.

"What the hell are you doing?" Valvano said. "I appreciate the gesture, but you need to do what is best for you, and it doesn't make any sense for you to transfer."

"He was the one who told me to stop all this nonsense," Corchiani says.

So, in the end, Corchiani and Monroe both returned for the senior seasons to play for first-year head coach Les Robinson. In turn, Robinson essentially turned the team over to his two captains and let them take the team as far as it would go.

"Every time I see Coach Robinson, I thank him for making our senior year something special."

[CHRIS CORCHIANI]

"Every time I see Coach Robinson, I thank him for making our senior year something special," Corchiani says.

Though they were roommates on the road for one season, Corchiani and Monroe say they weren't really as close during their college days as people assume. Generally, after games and practices, they went their separate ways.

But once their college careers ended, they became closer, as each pursued professional careers that took them to all points of the globe. Corchiani played in Italy, Turkey, Germany and Spain, as well as for the Orlando Magic, the Boston Celtics and the Washington Bullets. He has settled down in Raleigh now with his wife and five children, and has begun a career in residential real estate.

"Playing professionally was fun," Corchiani says. "I had been playing basketball my whole life, and I didn't want to stop. I thought it was a great opportunity for me financially and culturally, to see so many parts of the world."

He even adopted a son, while playing abroad in Turkey, something that gave Corchiani a connection to Herb Sendek's program when guard Engin Atsur was recruited to play for the Wolfpack and became the first Turkish native to play in the ACC.

Monroe began his career as a second-round pick of the Atlanta Hawks, but played only 38 games before being relegated to the vagabond life of a career professional player in Europe. He made stops in Australia, Israel and the Czech Republic, before settling down in the Italian leagues. He's been there since 1999 and plans to go back for the 2004-05 season.

It's not the kind of career that Monroe envisioned when he finished his Wolfpack career, but it has been financially rewarding.

"When I left N.C. State, I was expecting to be a high draft pick in the NBA," Monroe said. "People were telling me I would be a top-15 pick. That's what I expected, and I expected to play many years in the NBA.

"When I first went to Europe, I knew I could have a career playing basketball over there, but my goal was to play in the NBA. Sometimes things don't work that way."

Every summer for 10 years, however, Corchiani and Monroe returned to Raleigh to conduct the popular "Fire & Ice" basketball camps. They meet up on occasion now for family vacations. And at the beginning of the 2003-04 basketball season, they hooked up one more time on N.C. State's home court, to have their jerseys raised together in the rafters of the RBC Center.

JULIUS
HODGE

There was no doubt that Julius Hodge's family needed the money. The skinny swing guard from Harlem had too many memories of Christmas mornings with nothing more than a street vendor ALF doll as his only present and Easters spent at home in the family's apartment on West 151st Street.

"We couldn't afford any new clothes, so we didn't go out at Easter," Hodge says.

Ever since he was six years old, after learning the game from his big brother Steve at the Jackie Robinson Park basketball courts a block away from home, Hodge has been working to get his mother out of the city. Mary Hodge, a school cook at P.S. 192 with roots in North Carolina, raised three children on her own and made do by working more than one job when she had to. Sometimes, dinner consisted of little more than a bologna sandwich.

"My mom is the most beautiful woman in the world to me," Hodge says. "It's because of her character and how hard she worked to raise her family, which is not easy for a single black woman in Harlem."

But she also demanded more of her youngest son than just a little financial security. The paper she wanted to see was not green, but sheepskin.

When Hodge considered declaring himself eligible for the NBA draft following his junior season, Mary Hodge put her foot down. She wanted to see a college degree in his hands before a shoe contract.

"We've been poor our whole lives," she told him when he went home to make his final decision. "It won't kill us to wait another year."

JULIUS HODGE

Born: November 18, 1983
High School: St. Raymond's High School
Position: Guard
Number: 24
Years with the Wolfpack: 2001-05
NCAA Tournament Appearances: 2002, '03, '04
Honors:
★ 2001 McDonald's All-American
★ 2001 First-team Parade All-American
★ 2001 Mr. Basketball for New York
★ 2003, '04 First-team All-ACC selection
★ 2002 ACC All-Freshman team
★ 2002 Second-team All-ACC Tournament
★ 2003 First-team All-ACC Tournament
★ 2004 ACC Player of the Year

But she may have killed Julius if he had not continued to pursue his Bachelor of Arts degree in Communication.

"That was something she pretty much insisted on when he enrolled at North Carolina State," Steve Hodge said of his baby brother. "He had some thoughts of entering the draft after his junior year, but she said, 'You made a promise to me that you would get your degree, and that is what I want you to do.'"

Maybe it's too early to call Hodge a legend of Wolfpack basketball, since his career was not yet complete when this book was written. Heading into his final season of eligibility, he still had plenty of goals he wanted to achieve, both team and individual. He wanted to become the first guy since Wake Forest's Tim Duncan to win back-to-back ACC Player of the Year awards. He not only wanted to be named consensus All-America but also National Player of the Year.

"I don't see a player in college better than me."

[JULIUS HODGE]

He wanted desperately to lead the Wolfpack to an ACC title, something he believes he and his teammates let slip away in his sophomore season when they blew a second-half lead against Duke. And, more than anything, he wanted to win the school's third NCAA Championship.

That was his stated goal when he came to Raleigh as a skinny but extremely talented freshman, whose versatility on the court fit in perfectly with Herb Sendek's newly installed Princeton offense. Hodge, who had played all five positions in high school, proved to be capable at either guard position and as a small forward.

The Wolfpack was coming off its only losing season under Sendek, and rumors swirled about the coach's future with the program. It had been 10 years since the Wolfpack had been invited to the NCAA Tournament, and the fans of a school that had never gone more than nine years without an ACC championship were getting quite impatient about missing the Big Dance for more than a decade.

That changed quickly with the arrival of Hodge's freshman class. He joined little-known forward Ilian Evitmov, Josh Powell, Jordan Collins and Levi Watkins for what was hailed as clearly the best recruiting class in the ACC. With leadership provided by first-team All-ACC guard Anthony Grundy and fifth-year senior Archie Miller, the Wolfpack ended its NCAA drought by upsetting eventual national champion Maryland in the ACC Tournament semifinals and advancing to the championship game.

But in each of Hodge's first three trips to the NCAA, the team has suffered disappointing, even disheartening, losses. As a freshman, it was against Connecticut, as a sophomore against California, and a junior against Vanderbilt. He believes his senior season will be different, especially as he surveys the college basketball landscape around him.

"I don't see a player in college better than me," Hodge says candidly.

It was a trying journey, filled with snow-covered nights on the basketball court at Jackie Robinson and long hours of after-midnight shooting at Reynolds Coliseum, to get to that point.

Throughout his youth and college career, Hodge's family lived in a six-story apartment building in Uptown Harlem, a rough neighborhood by anyone's standards.

"There were the drugs, the gunshots being fired at night, things of that nature," says Steve Hodge, who is eight years older than his brother. "It's just not an easy place to live. But it also helped Julius mature quicker than other people, and it helped his character."

Julius Hodge has met his father, but he has no relationship with him. Steve, who played at Sullivan County Community College in Manhattan and then at Division II Southampton College on Long Island for two years, was his strongest male influence, and his positive role model kept Julius on the right path.

"It's easy to get distracted where I am from," Hodge says. "People think there are three ways you can get out of there: play sports, go to school or sell drugs."

Many young men take the latter path, which is by far the easiest. Hodge has always taken the toughest road, by working tirelessly on his game from the time he decided that basketball was the way to get his family out of harm's way.

Hodge has never strayed from the goal he set as a young kid, when he told his mother, "I am going to use this ball to get us out of here." That's when he decided, like so many other wide-eyed youths, that he wanted to become an NBA star. Not just a professional player, a star.

"My goal still is to be in the NBA Hall of Fame," Hodge says, with no hint that this might be an unattainable quest.

So far, nothing has derailed that dream. Not the hour-long commute he made every day from the eighth grade until his senior year in high school from Harlem to the Bronx, where he attended St. Raymond's High School. He got a scholarship to the private school after attending camp there twice in middle school.

But it was not exactly an easy education. Every morning he was a student at St.

Raymond's, Hodge got up between 5 to 5:30 a.m. He took four teeth-rattling subway trains from Harlem to the Bronx and walked seven blocks to get to school. After he made friends with the school janitors, he always got to school at least an hour before classes started so he could work on his jumpshot in the school gym.

The constant transit took its toll. After his fifth year of making that daily commute, capping off his career by leading the school to the Federation A city and state championships, Hodge was tired of the urban way of life.

"I had to get away from New York City," says Hodge, who could have gone to Syracuse instead of N.C. State. "There was just too much that could happen there."

After a senior season in which he was named McDonald's and Parade All-America, Hodge made the surprising announcement that he was going to play for the Wolfpack, heading back to the state where his mother was born near Wilson. He came into the ACC as the league's highest rated freshman in 2001.

Hodge never strayed from his tireless workout regimen. When he got to Raleigh, he outworked everyone on the roster. In the summers, he would put about six hours a day into his game. He rarely ever took any time off, which is why his skinny frame couldn't keep any meat on it, despite his attempts to lift weights and eat pizza after pizza.

Frequently, during the season, Hodge would get off the bus following a road game, and head straight to the practice gym, get-

"He's just a hard worker.
There is really no other way to put it."

[STEVE HODGE]

ting in another 1,500 or so shots before going to bed.

"He's just a hard worker," Steve Hodge says. "There is really no other way to put it."

Wolfpack coach Herb Sendek has seen other workaholics over the years, including in the mirror. Hodge is among the hardest working players he has ever been around.

"He is extremely driven," Sendek says. "He cares a great deal about basketball. He works very hard at it. With all his heart, he wants to do well. You can never question his intent."

He brought an aggressively playful Harlem attitude to Herb Sendek's frequently buttoned-down program, one that didn't always sit well with opposing fans. Only a few games into his freshman year, Hodge was dancing a jig on the sidelines at Syracuse, as the Wolfpack upset the Top 10 Orangemen, a team that was a finalist among Hodge's college choices. He did something similar three games later at Virginia, and earned the designation, from at least one of the down south newspapers, as the ACC's Most Annoying Player.

"I draw energy from the crowd," Hodge says as his only defense.

But Hodge's brash personality also signaled to the rest of the ACC that the Wolfpack program had returned from its dol-

drums of the 1990s, when coaching transitions, academic reforms in the wake of Jim Valvano's resignation and other changes in the athletics department combined to put State at the bottom of the ACC standings.

Hodge, whose flair for dramatics helped him get a concentration in theater with his communications degree, has tickled Wolfpack fans with his sharp tongue. Like the time he said of the Duke crowd: "I am not going to let a kid with a 4.5 GPA, acne and bad breath determine how I play."

Some people will never let him forget what he said as a freshman, about the slower life down South.

"It's kind of slow," Hodge said to a handful of reporters. "Being in New York, I could wake up at three in the morning and decide to go to the store and there would be like cars racing down the street and people walking around everywhere. If I do that here, I'll probably get attacked by a deer or something."

"I draw energy
from the crowd."

[JULIUS HODGE]

"It was just standing on the side of the road. I just stopped and stared. My girl-friend looked at me like I was crazy and said, 'What are you doing?'"

[JULIUS HODGE]

Hodge finally did run across a deer, not long after his junior year while driving through a rural part of the state late one night with his girlfriend. It's often been said that there are two kind of drivers in North Carolina: those who have hit a deer and those who haven't—yet. But Hodge didn't do the attacking.

"It was just standing on the side of the road," Hodge says. "I just stopped and stared. My girlfriend looked at me like I was crazy and said, 'What are you doing?'"

"I just kind of wanted to take it in for a few minutes."

And, in the end, those were the kind of priceless learning experiences that Mary Hodge wanted her son to have before he went bounding off to professional basketball.

Celebrate the Heroes of North Carolina Sports

and College Basketball in These Other 2004 Releases from Sports Publishing!

Tales from the Carolina Panthers Sideline
by Scott Fowler

- 5.5 x 8.25 hardcover
- 200 pages
- photos throughout
- $19.95

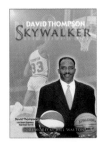

David Thompson: Skywalker
by David Thompson with Sean Stormes and Marshall Terrill

- 6 x 9 hardcover
- 8-page b/w photo insert
- 279 pages • $22.95

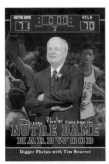

Digger Phelps's Tales from the Notre Dame Hardwood
by Digger Phelps with Tim Bourret

- 5.5 x 8.25 hardcover
- 30 photos throughout
- 200+ pages • $19.95

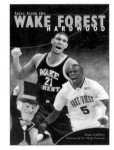

Tales from the Wake Forest Hardwood
by Dan Collins

- 5.5 x 8.25 hardcover
- 200 pages
- photos throughout
- $19.95

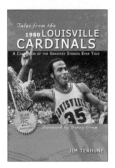

Tales from the 1980 Louisville Cardinals
by Jim Terhune

- 5.5 x 8.25 hardcover
- 200 pages
- 25-30 photos throughout
- $19.95

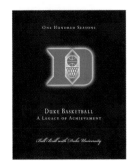

100 Years of Duke Basketball: A Legacy of Achievement
by Bill Brill

- 9 x 12 hardcover
- 240+ pages
- 140 photos throughout
- $29.95

The Indiana University Basketball Encyclopedia
by Jason Hiner

- 8.5 x 11 hardcover
- 250+ photos throughout plus full-color panoramic foldout
- 500+ pages • $49.95

Legends of Maryland Basketball
by Dave Ungrady

- 8.5 x 11 hardcover
- 160+ pages
- color photos throughout
- $24.95

Dale Brown's Memoirs from LSU Basketball
by Dale Brown

- 6 x 9 hardcover
- 184 pages
- photos throughout
- $24.95

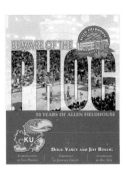

Beware of the Phog: 50 Years of Allen Fieldhouse
by Doug Vance and Jeff Bollig

- 9 x 12 hardcover
- 160+ pages
- 140 color photos throughout
- $29.95

To order at any time, please call toll-free **877-424-BOOK (2665)**.
For fast service and quick delivery, order on-line at **www.SportsPublishingLLC.com.**